Dear Verna,

Thank you for being
an ongoing inspiration.

Best,

Shari. 4/05.

# Doing Nothing is Not an Option!

*Facing the Imminent Labor Crisis*

Robert K. Critchley

THOMSON

™

SOUTH-WESTERN

Australia · Canada · Mexico · Singapore · Spain · United Kingdom · United States

## THOMSON
## SOUTH-WESTERN

*Doing Nothing is Not an Option*
Robert K. Critchley

**Vice President/**
**Editorial Director**
Jack Calhoun

**Vice President/**
**Editor-in-Chief**
Dave Shaut

**Acquisitions**
**Editor**
Steve Momper

**Channel Manager, Retail**
Chris McNamee

**Channel Manager,**
**Professional**
Mark Linton

**Production Manager**
Patricia Matthews Boies

**Production Editor**
Darrell E. Frye

**Manufacturing Coordinator**
Charlene Taylor

**Senior Designer**
Mike Stratton

**Compositor**
Navta Associates, Inc.

**Printer**
Phoenix Book Technology
Hagerstown, MD

Critchley, Robert K.
  Doing nothing is not an option! : facing the imminent labor crisis / Robert Critchley.
    p. cm.
  Includes bibliographical references and index.
  ISBN 0-324-22326-9 (alk. paper)
  1. Labor supply. 2. Work environment. 3. Older people—Employment. I. Title.
  HD5706.C75 2004
  658.3'01—dc22                                              2004022759

International Division List

**ASIA (Including India):**
Thomson Learning
60 Albert Street, #15-01
Albert Complex
Singapore 189969
Tel 65 336-6411
Fax 65 336-7411

**AUSTRALIA/NEW ZEALAND:**
Nelson
102 Dodds Street
South Melbourne
Victoria 3205
Australia
Tel 61 (0)3 9685-4111
Fax 61 (0)3 9685-4199

**LATIN AMERICA:**
Thomson Learning
Seneca 53
Colonia Polanco
11560 Mexico, D.F. Mexico
Tel (525) 281-2906
Fax (525) 281-2656

**CANADA:**
Nelson
1120 Birchmount Road
Toronto, Ontario
Canada M1K 5G4
Tel (416) 752-9100
Fax (416) 752-8102

**UK/EUROPE/MIDDLE EAST/AFRICA:**
Thomson Learning
Berkshire House
168-173 High Holborn
London WC1V 7AA
United Kingdom
Tel 44 (0)20 497-1422
Fax 44 (0)20 497-1426

**SPAIN (includes Portugal):**
Paraninfo
Calle Magallanes 25
28015 Madrid
España
Tel 34 (0)91 446-3350
Fax 34 (0)91 445-6218

**Contents**

# Contents

## DEDICATION

"To Cooper, Jaxson, and Jaydon,
for keeping their Grandfather young at heart.
May all their dreams come true."

Robert Critchley is a Strategic Workforce Consultant who partners with organisations to gain competitive advantage by leveraging the talents of their multigenerational workforce.

Previously he was International President for DBM Inc., a leading Outplacement and Career Management Company with operations in 51 countries, responsible for global operations outside of North America. This role evolved from his success as President of the Asia Pacific Region. He started and developed the DBM business as a licensee in Australia and later sold it to the US parent.

Earlier in his career, he spent over 20 years in the banking industry, primarily in Australia and the UK, and also started and developed a very successful Management Consultancy specializing in strategic planning, and corporate restructuring.

He currently holds Chairman and Director roles with several companies listed on the Australian Stock Exchange covering diverse industries. He also plays an active role in supporting charitable institutions and not for profit organizations.

Also written by the Author: *Rewired, Rehired or Retired? A Global Guide for the Experienced Worker*—(John Wiley & Sons Inc, 2002)

# Acknowledgments

M any people have provided inspiration and support for this book. I appreciate their very positive contributions towards its creation and thank them very much.

This book has become a reality due to the totally focused, passionate, and dedicated efforts of Jodi Storey. As with "Rewired, Rehired or Retired?," Jodi became fully immersed in the project, and her detailed research, anecdotes, creativity, and wonderful turn of phrase converted my storyline into a far more enjoyable and completed work. Jodi was totally committed throughout the project with a dedication to achieving perfection, continually improving the content, and I give her my heartfelt thanks. Jodi has put in an amazing effort, and this book would have still been a "work in progress" if not for her drive, determination and pursuit of excellence.

Thank you to Shari Fryer for her wonderful encouragement, passion for the project, and creative input. From her base in the United States, she has provided invaluable information to ensure all concepts and information were current as well as giving a contemporary, macro-point of view. Her remarkable understanding of business principles, people in transition, marketing strategies, and maximizing profitability has brought another valuable dimension to this book. I would also like to thank her husband, Darrin, for his creativity and continuous support for the project, and to both of them for the great ideas and suggestions that came from a very memorable drive to Wyoming.

Merilyn, my wife, has once again been a constant source of support, providing keen observations and feedback, and has shown great patience and tolerance for my absentmindedness while in writing mode. For this, I thank her greatly. Both Merilyn and I have gained great pride throughout this project from witnessing the achievements of our daughters, Jodi and Shari, and how they continue to teach us new things.

My sincere appreciation and respect goes to Steve Momper, my Publisher, who embraced the project with much passion, gave me a free hand, and totally supported this book. I thank him for his clear understanding of where the journey was going as well as his constructive input along the way. Steve made the process very enjoyable. I would also like to give special thanks to Steve's colleagues at South Western, Mark Linton, Cathy Coleman, Darrell Frye, Chris McNamee, and Tippy McIntosh.

My original introduction to Steve came from my friends at Thomson Corporation, Steve Mower, and Bebe Pierce, who truly embraced the messages I had conveyed in *Rewired, Rehired or Retired?* and suggested I meet with Steve Momper. I thank them for their belief in my passion.

Thanks to my good friend Craig Sawin, CEO of Novations Inc. who reviewed the raw manuscript and provided excellent input and feedback.

Special thanks also go to my Assistant, Lyn Tarbuck, for her contribution of ideas and research, and providing me with top class administrative support in such a manner of ease and excellence.

A number of people provided case study support for the book and I would like to especially thank Caroline Waters from British Telecom, Steve Mower from Thomson Corporation (again), Malcolm Jackman and Colin Shaw from Coates Hire, Martin Whittaker and Guy Pearce from Cordukes, and Cherie Romaro from Foxtel/Austar who all shared so many valuable insights into their organizations so that others could learn and prosper. I appreciate their time and enthusiasm for the project.

Thank you to my good friends, who are past and present employees of DBM, who provided valuable input and encouragement including Vicky Bloch, Maureen Sullivan, Peter Tobin, Tad Otsuki, Pat Burke, Derek Wetterling, and Linda Neville. I also thank Tim Hessell and Anthony Gavan for their support.

I would also like to acknowledge those wonderful people around the world who I have had the pleasure to assist with their career and life planning while in transition on DBM Outplacement programs, enabling me to gain a true understanding of their experiences.

Throughout my journey of researching and writing this book—a book that aspires to a better world of work and living—I have encountered so many discreditable examples of what is actually occurring in the world of work today. Unwittingly, those people responsible have provided me with the inspiration and motivation to write Doing Nothing is Not an Option!

—*Robert K Critchley*

# Foreword

At a time when high unemployment rates make the headlines regularly, Robert Critchley's prediction of a severe labor shortage ahead may seem counterintuitive. But Critchley is no wild-eyed futurist. He points to trends that every CEO should note well.

Critchley explains clearly what the aging population in developed countries means for employers:

*With approximately 60 million baby boomers potentially leaving the workforce throughout the next 15 years and fewer young people joining to replace them, there will be a significant void in available leadership talent.*

The rapid growth of the older population and the rapid decline of the younger generation will create new challenges for all sorts of organizations.

For corporations, the key challenge will be creating a work environment that enables older workers to remain motivated, engaged and productive longer—while at the same time attracting, developing and retaining younger workers in an increasingly competitive job market. The needs and behaviors of these two workforces—the over-50s and the under-30s—will be quite distinct.

Importantly, Critchley lays out what Human Resources departments must do *now* to ensure that tomorrow's workforce is not just grayer than today's—but also more productive. Managing the multigenerational workforce of the next decade will require not only new HR policies and approaches, but also new leadership skills.

Many companies already recognize that changing demographics will soon impact their employee base in unprecedented ways. And they're questioning what to do about it. These forward-looking companies will welcome Critchley's advice on how to ride the winds of change rather than getting blown away by them.

Not only is the composition of the workforce changing, but so is the nature of work itself. As the technology revolution continues, a higher percentage of employees in industrialized nations are becoming knowledge workers. That puts a high premium on education and on-the-job training. Knowledge workers of all ages must be provided with the training and the productivity tools they need to succeed in an ever-changing market.

And licensing and certification will be essential to distinguish those who keep their skills current from those who fall behind on the perpetual learning curve.

While the pace of technological change will not slacken, careers will grow longer. More and more people will keep working well into what used to be called "retirement age." Put those two facts together and it is clear that lifelong learning will be integral to the 21st century workplace. Workers pursuing fifty-year careers will need to update their skills regularly, if not reskill entirely, to remain competitive. Indeed, *The Economist* recently reported that "The fastest-growing industry in any developed country may turn out to be the continuing education of already well-educated adults."

As a CEO, I don't lie awake nights worrying about the companies that compete with mine. Instead, I lie awake wondering what more I can do to ensure that my company continues to have the right people with the right skills in the right jobs. In my business, as in many other companies in the growing knowledge industry, the core value is people. The only sustainable competitive advantage comes from the expertise, drive and integrity of our employees. I know that if we are better at talent management than the competition, we will win in the marketplace.

As Critchley points out, "no company ever went bankrupt because it suffered from having too much talent."

Richard J. Harrington
President & Chief Executive Officer
The Thomson Corporation

# Prologue

The past decade has been tough for many, and not even the most profitable organizations in the world today cannot guarantee their own ongoing existence, let alone provide stability for their employees.

There is a tidal wave of change occurring within today's workplace due to dynamic demographic changes, yet many organizations and their leaders are oblivious to the consequences and are not implementing necessary strategies for future survival.

The following statistics highlight significant changes developing within the demographic mix of our workforce:

- In 2010 there will be 168 million jobs in the United States but only 158 million workers to undertake them (a shortfall of 10 million workers).
- The number of employees in the 25–34 age group dropped nearly 8 percent during the 1990s.
- Older workers will comprise 17 percent of the total workforce in 2010, up from 13 percent in 2000 (a dramatic shift in a decade).
- The number of workers aged 55 or older (which totaled 18.2 million in 2000) is projected to rise to 25.3 million in 2008, which will increase the median age of the workforce to 41, compared to 38 in 1998 and 34 in 1978.

Unless this fundamental shift in the demographics of our workforce is acknowledged, understood, and addressed swiftly, future viability and success will be seriously at risk.

Creative employment strategies and practices must be embraced to retain and motivate workers of all ages. Otherwise, as the workforce shrinks, there will not be enough people with the necessary skills to ensure ongoing growth and productivity. By the time many organizations acknowledge the implications of not having enough workers, it may be too late to recover.

## Doing nothing is *NOT* an option!

Some CEOs offer excuses for not being aware of these crucial workplace issues or feel trapped because of significant pressure from shareholders, media, and investor groups to perform in semiannual, or even quarterly, intervals. CEOs who focus only on short-term planning horizons condemn their organizations to mediocrity and future substandard performance. There will be significant consequences for those who don't react appropriately to the imminent changes taking place.

We can no longer resort to past practices alone to inspire and save us due to the fact we are currently entering unchartered waters. Now, out of necessity, employees are transforming from a position of enfeeblement to one of enlightenment and are taking control of their future rather than relying on their employer.

We must adopt new, dynamic approaches that engage and motivate our aging workforce while, at the same time, promote innovation and productivity in our younger workers in order to prevent staff shrinkage, unwanted turnover, and lowered productivity. Both short-term and long-term employment strategies that are well researched and achievable must be urgently embraced for ongoing productivity.

Over the past ten years, there have been significant levels of merger and acquisition activity resulting in large fallout of surplus employees as a result of rationalization efforts. Over the last four years, in particular, there has been a slowdown in global economic activity, resulting in high levels of unemployment. This has contributed to complacency by employers, wrongly concluding there will be a never-ending stream of available workers to fill future workforce requirements. The reality of declining workforce numbers has been disguised, and the impact is only now revealing itself.

In our modern age of enhanced technology and automation, many business leaders ignore or underrate the importance of recruiting and retaining good people. Yet corporate leaders today must focus primarily on the human composition of their organization if they are to survive and prosper. Increased and sustainable profitability is likely to follow if a work environment is created where:

- All workers understand, believe in, and support the organization's vision, particularly in times of change;
- Corporate and personal goals are aligned via effective communication;
- Flexible work arrangements are provided;
- There is a multigenerational and diverse workforce;
- There is an environment of trust; and
- Talented people wish to remain and are motivated to make a worthwhile contribution.

*Change before you have to.*
Jack Welch, Former CEO & Chairman of General Electric

We are now facing a two-sided dilemma where, on the one hand, many individuals are retiring earlier than originally planned, either voluntarily or involuntarily, and are leaving the workforce at 50, 55, or 60, rather than the previous retirement age of 65. However, in most countries, people are now living longer and healthier lives (and are therefore capable of working longer) than previous generations, and our perception of old age is shifting.

**This is the first generation ever to have reached their 50s largely unscathed from war, disease, or famine.**

On the other hand, many younger people have chosen not to marry, or to marry later in life and to have no children or fewer children than their parents, creating a shortfall in population numbers. The never-ending pool of young talent to recruit and develop within our organizations (that we have been used to over the past 30 years) is now drying up.

Over the past decade, so many organizations faced with cost cutting have pushed their 'over 50' workers out the door first. These fat-trimming actions, however, have been detrimental to many companies as they have lost valuable experience and much needed personnel to sustain future growth and profitability.

Suggested short-term, Band-Aid solutions to alleviate the need for more workers include increasing immigration and/or outsourcing services to lower-cost countries and to replace workers with technology wherever possible. However, they are only partial solutions that do not solve the problem totally, as immigration can only grow at a controlled rate (to avoid social and economic integration difficulties) and many jobs are too specialized or localized to be outsourced to other countries.

My motivation to write this book stemmed from my research and the discovery that many of today's business leaders need and want to find better ways to address workforce challenges. Following the launch of my book *Rewired, Rehired, or Retired?* (published in 2002 by John Wiley & Sons Inc.), I embarked on a global roadshow to meet with business leaders and human resource professionals. This experience, combined with my learnings from working with hundreds of individuals undergoing career transition, enabled me to have a unique umbrella perspective of what people of all ages seek within their careers today as well as how effectively organizations are responding. My assessment was that further improvement was required by many organizations to create more meaningful and effective HR strategies.

While *Rewired, Rehired, or Retired?* focused on career and life strategies for older workers, I have written this book to assist CEOs and human resource professionals to deploy creative employment practices to leverage the talents (and reap the benefits) of their multigenerational workforces.

The strategies to face the impending labor crisis and maximize opportunities for success, which are shared in this book, are sourced from my research, as well as from my own very diverse business and life experiences. From my observations, it is painfully clear that the following workplace issues require urgent attention:

- Few organizations truly understand (or have addressed) the dramatic demographic shift currently occurring.
- The effects of the aging workforce are either misunderstood or ignored because focus is placed on other immediate issues that are considered more critical.
- Many employers are unaware of the demographic mix of talent within their own workforce.
- Replacement of workers retiring within the next five years has not been fully considered.
- Limited thought has been given to effective recruitment and retention of future leaders.
- The impact of not having sufficient workers to achieve optimum productivity in the future has not been acknowledged.

---

55 percent of companies polled have no plan in place to either attract or retain workers aged 50 and over.

DBM Research, July 2002

---

This book provides a unique and timely insight into each working generation's psyche, attitudes, and desires and is drawn from extensive interaction with corporations around the globe who have recently gone through or are undergoing change. The many amazing people I have been privileged to meet and coach who are going through career transition have given me a great opportunity to understand what motivates them. I also believe I am empathetic with organizational leaders who are obliged to outwardly display passion, excitement, and drive, yet inwardly experience fear, uncertainty, and frustration (usually leading to stress, lack of fulfillment and sometimes illness).

Consider your current work environment. Which of the following scenarios do you most closely identify with?

## Scenario 1

Morale and motivation among employees of all ages couldn't be better. Recruiting and retaining high-performing individuals is easy due to effective management, mentoring, and flexible workplace conditions. You are fully aware of the demographics of your workplace, workers of all ages are valued, and you are preparing now for an aging workforce. Your organization is flourishing and is deemed an "employer of choice."

## Scenario 2

You feel as if you are running faster and faster on a treadmill, yet are only making sluggish progress. Achieving and maintaining profitability is a struggle, and recruiting, motivating, and retaining good people is an ongoing challenge. There is constant pressure to perform within shorter time frames, with increasingly limited resources because of high staff turnover. Older workers are rarely promoted, and workers of all ages fear for their jobs, as trust no longer exists. Your organization is not viewed as an industry leader or a desirable employer.

If Scenario 1 accurately describes your workplace, your days are obviously filled with enjoyment and satisfaction and you are confident of continued corporate and personal success. Congratulations! You are the envy of many.

If, however, you relate more to Scenario 2, it is my sincere hope you will benefit greatly from the information I share with you in this book. You are among the vast majority of individuals around the world who are now facing a multitude of diverse and frustrating challenges within the workplace, including the realization that unless we change current work practices to encourage older employees to continue working rather than retiring, and create work environments to attract and retain younger workers, there will be more people leaving the workforce than joining over the next decade.

I have met a large number of people from around the world who have experienced involuntary transition after losing their jobs. In particular, while writing *Rewired, Rehired, or Retired?*, I heard many shocking stories of how badly organizations treated their departing employees, no matter how long they'd been employed. There are a large number of employers throughout the world who have destroyed trust by focusing on short-term solutions at the expense of long-term objectives.

In the following chapters, I have developed a blueprint for leaders to work through the challenges of tomorrow's workplace, with clear concepts and strategies that can be readily adapted and implemented into your organization. It is my aim to provide CEOs, HR professionals, and business leaders with the necessary tools to address and prepare for this impending crisis and to minimize potential detrimental effects.

Most importantly, every suggestion made in this book is a low-cost or no-cost method for companies to address their responsibilities, with the goal of achieving positive fiscal outcomes. What is required, however, is a fresh attitude to address these issues and the courage to implement necessary strategies.

Throughout this book I will assist you to chart a course through these turbulent times, ensuring survival and optimizing long-term prosperity for your organization and for you as an individual.

The challenge for business leaders today is to deal effectively with an older workforce while, at the same time, nurture their shrinking pool of younger, more independent workers, to leverage the strengths of their talent resources as a whole and to maximize performance. Corporate leaders must focus on providing flexibility to the human contribution within their organization if they are to survive and prosper.

This imminent labor crisis must be faced head-on in order to minimize negative effects and to create a sound foundation of passionate, dedicated employees within a flexible, supportive environment. Only then can we sustain and optimize corporate profits, achieve a winning workplace and be regarded by current and potential employees as an employer of choice. So many aspire to this, but sadly, few organizations actually achieve it.

**In today's workplace, the only sustainable differentiator is an organization's people.**

**Doing nothing is NOT an option!**

---

*Long-range planning does not deal with future decisions, but with the future of present decisions.*
Peter Drucker, Management Consultant & Author

---

# The Road Ahead

**Crumbling Paradise**

---

*The times they are a-changin'.*
Bob Dylan, Singer & Songwriter

---

The world of work is now entering a dramatic, unprecedented period of change. We are on the verge of new territory and can no longer refer to our history books. Retrospection of management theories and HR strategies that have prevailed in the past is now of limited use.

A business world that was once familiar, rational, and predictable has become confusing, irrational and illogical. If you are contemplating any type of change in your own career today, you'll need to make your plans in the context of the broad change swirling about you.

When many of us entered the workforce, we joined organizations that shared the common and simple career policy of "Leave it to us." If we did our job and remained loyal to our employers, we expected them to look after us. It could even mean a "job for life."

We have all witnessed substantial change within our workplace structures over the past decade or so due to a global recession in the early years of the 21st century, coupled with the vast amount of merger and acquisition activity during the last decade of the 20th century. With much focus on maintaining short-term existence, gaining a competitive advantage, and penetrating global markets, organizations have dangerously failed to notice an underlying trend in the demographics of our global workforce.

*To exist is to change, to change is to mature, to mature is to go on creating oneself endlessly.*
Henry Bergson, French Philosopher & Nobel Laureate

Until recently, organizations have enjoyed picking and choosing from a never-ending pool of willing candidates who were prepared to align themselves with corporate goals. Generally, it has been an employer's paradise with large numbers of potential employees from which to select.

You may have experienced a shortage of suitable people with the specific skill set required from time to time. However, in both good and tough times, there has always been a steady supply of young people joining the ranks of the workforce from schools or colleges, far exceeding the number of those retiring from the workforce. Because of this, there has often been limited regard or respect for sustaining an employee's motivation and satisfaction, particularly if the employee's specific career goals weren't completely in sync with the goals of the corporation.

It would, of course, be unfair to suggest that all organizations have been arrogant in their dealings with staff. There have been many successful examples of companies respecting their employees and aspiring to create a winning workplace and be an employer of choice.

All employers must now appreciate the importance of recognizing and nurturing each individual's contribution in order to face the challenge of retaining key people. Today's workforce is multifaceted and is comprised of the following generational categories:

| GENERATION | WHEN THEY WERE BORN |
|---|---|
| Matures | 1945 or earlier |
| Baby Boomers | 1946–1964 |
| Generation X | 1965–1980 |
| Generation Y | 1981 or later |

In writing my previous book *Rewired, Rehired, or Retired?*, the focus was largely on encouraging and guiding the experienced individual to achieve an edifying work/life balance, to maximize their potential in the workforce, ensuring they "lead their life, not follow it." That is, *Rewired, Rehired, or Retired?* addressed issues of employee satisfaction. Throughout this book, many of the same issues are addressed from an organizational perspective. Organizations must initiate policies and create a climate in which older employees can productively contribute, while, at the same time, nurture and retain younger workers in a changing environment where the employer's paradise is crumbling.

## Impending Shortfall

*More than 61 million Americans will retire during the next 30 years.*
Employment Policy Foundation Report, 2001

Throughout the past decade in particular, we have witnessed people retiring at an earlier age. Standards of living in the developed world are at higher levels than ever before, and many people who have built up adequate retirement savings have chosen to work less or not at all.

Since the baby boom following WWII, managers have worked on a theory that assumes an unlimited supply of enthusiastic young talent available to join their organizations. However, nowadays we have moved from an economy of free resources to one of scarce resources.

Regrettably, the value of the experienced worker has been ignored in many organizations, resulting in little money allocated to their training and development. There has been a pervading attitude of "They have little to contribute" or "They won't be with us long enough to recoup our investment." Because of this, experienced workers have often been viewed as dispensable and are usually the first ones laid off when a downsizing occurs and therefore pushed into involuntary retirement.

In addition, we are now experiencing a decline in fertility rates in most western industrialized countries. Progressively, over the last 20 years, more people have chosen or have been forced to have fewer (or no) children (and usually at a much older age) than their parents' generation. In fact, the United Nations has recently warned (in their Fertility Rates Report, February 2003) that the average fertility rate will decline to 1.85 by 2050, dangerously lower than the replacement rate of 2.1 per couple to maintain a stationary population level.

As the World Bank's website puts it: "No social phenomenon has attracted, more attention in the past half century than the 'population explosion'—that surge from about 2.5 billion people in 1950 to more than 6 billion in 1999, making the 20th century one of unprecedented population growth. As the number of people grew, the interval for adding another billion people became shorter and shorter, with the increase from 5 billion to 6 billion occurring in only 12 years." The world passed the 6 billion mark in 1999. The world's overall population growth rate is currently about 1.5 percent per year.

Recent analysis suggests that the world's peak population will likely be less than 9 billion, perhaps as low as 8 billion. We're looking at less than a 50 percent increase over today's global population over the next 45 years or so.

The World Bank projects that the 7 billion mark will be reached in 2014. Whatever the exact date, the current period marks the first time since the global population reached one billion that adding the next billion people took longer than the previous billion.

What this means is that the global population train has its brakes on hard, but it has taken a while for the train to scrub off momentum. In fact, 1997 marked the year of fastest population growth (90 million additional people) and the point at which the population train started slowing down (85 million for 1999, 80 million for 2000). From here on out, world population growth will be slower every year until the human population peaks—expected sometime around the year 2040 to 2050. Then the global population is expected to begin shrinking.

Fertility rates are always low in affluent countries. This is because in a developed country children are just plain expensive. Disposable diapers, Nike™ sneakers, car insurance, college tuition—I'm sure many of you can attest to exactly how expensive life in a developed economy can be. Women in the workplace mean that childcare, once a "free" commodity, is a major household expense. As a result, women in high-income countries now average only 1.7 children apiece.

Today, because of rapid economic growth and rising affluence, fertility rates have plummeted across the globe—most dramatically in formerly poor countries. The middle and lower income countries in the world together now average only 2.9 births per woman. The average fertility rate globally is now only 2.7 and falling, meaning that humanity has moved more than 75 percent of the way to a stabilizing fertility rate in only one generation. Moreover, fertility rates are still falling rapidly in virtually all developing countries.

Alex A. Avery, "World Market Drivers and Future Trends of Agriculture," Center for Global Food Issues, Hudson Institute

The explosive growth of the world's population experienced over the last 40 years is abating and now heading for decline in many countries as the following examples indicate:

- In Australia in 1961, the average number of children per female was 3.7, and in 2000 had reduced to 1.7 children.
- In Singapore in 1970, there was an average of 4 children per female, and this is now moving down towards 2 children.
- Thailand's fertility rate has dropped from 5 in the 1970s to just fewer than 2 in 2003.
- In Iran, women had 6.5 children each on average in the 1980s and are now only averaging 2.75.
- In Hong Kong, the decline is even more startling, with a dramatically low average today of 0.93 children per female.
- The average in Italy is now only 1.2 children per woman.
- In the world's most populous country, China, a "one child" policy now applies.

The net effect of these changes within our organizations is that more people will be leaving the workforce over the next decade than will actually join, unless current employment strategies are modified.

---

*In times of change, the learners shall inherit the earth, while the learned find themselves beautifully equipped to deal with a world that no longer exists.*
Eric Hoffer, Author & Philosopher

---

Over the next ten years, employers will face the brand-new dilemma of having a very limited pool of young talent to readily recruit and develop. The vast options that will become available to younger workers will enable them to be more selective and therefore make it more difficult for employers to successfully bid for their talent. Even if successful, there will be ongoing challenges for organizations to modify employment policies to retain these younger workers.

After being in the luxurious position of having too many workers for available jobs, there is now an ominous reversal occurring. As the graph below illustrates, we are now facing a shortfall of over 10 million workers by 2010 in the United States.

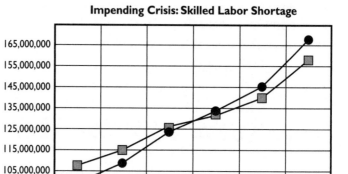

**Impending Crisis: Skilled Labor Shortage**

| | 1980 | 1985 | 1990 | 1995 | 2000 | 2010 |
|---|---|---|---|---|---|---|
| ● Jobs Available | 99,303,000 | 109,680,000 | 124,324,000 | 134,959,000 | 145,594,000 | 167,754,000 |
| ■ Civilian Labor Force | 106,940,000 | 115,461,000 | 125,840,000 | 132,304,000 | 140,863,000 | 157,721,000 |

Source: BLS Research 2001

As we can see from the above graph, up until 1990 there were more people available than jobs to fill, making it possible for employers to be selective. Since the early 1990s this position has been reversed, and there are now more jobs available than people to fill them.

Back in 2000 when there were approximately 4.5 million more jobs than workers, we continued with normal workplace strategies without noticing the need for changing the rules. There was a higher rate of unemployment, outsourcing was becoming a common practice, and the lack of available workers wasn't viewed as a potential long-term crisis. However, the labor shortage is now gathering speed, and we must address necessary employment planning modifications. As the labor shortage approaches 10 million people at the end of this decade, this turn of events will become critical.

## Ostrich Mentality

*He that will not apply new remedies must expect new evils.*
Francis Bacon, English Philosopher

If we do not carefully handle this situation in the immediate short-term, the hard truth is that organizations will face the crisis of not having enough people to sustain future growth and profitability. CEOs who have not considered this rapidly changing environment most certainly have not considered the consequences of their inaction. Corporate survival will depend on how well these issues are addressed.

In many cases, organizations are either not aware or are choosing to ignore this phenomenon. Alarmingly, by the time they acknowledge the reality of not having enough workers, it may be too late to recover.

Some multinationals that recognize the potential deficiency in available personnel are focusing on outsourcing to other countries where labor is enticingly cheaper. There are numerous instances of companies setting up operations in lower-cost countries, employing skilled and educated workers for software development, call centers and data processing, for example, in countries such as Malaysia, China and India. In fact, it has been estimated that approximately four million jobs will have moved from the United States to India by 2008.

---

Cheaper telecommunications are allowing businesses to easily outsource part of their operations, reducing costs by as much as 50 percent. The Indian Government offers incentives to set up operations, including subsidies and free rent.

There are more than 200,000 workers in India, most of them with university degrees, working for offshore companies. They earn an average of $5,175 a year.

Jim O'Rourke, "Indian Group's Bid to Grab our White-Collar Jobs," *The Sun-Herald*, March 14, 2004

---

This attempt at solving the problem of less available talent still does not overcome the fact that:

- Not all jobs can be outsourced (especially the jobs being vacated), for example, someone to open the shop, serve the customers, clean the premises, and deliver the goods.
- Not all jobs can be filled by immigrants as there are restrictions on the number that can be successfully absorbed annually in each country, from socioeconomic and cultural points of view, to ensure long-term successful assimilation; and
- Not everyone can be replaced by technology.

Nearly a quarter of the labor shortage (23.5 percent) could be eliminated by increasing annual immigration levels by 300,000 individuals, from 980,000 to 1,280,000 per year. Though raising immigration levels slightly would not be a complete solution, taken together with improved labor force participation rates for older men, and sustained levels of higher productivity, immigration could play a significant role in addressing the problem.

The Employment Policy Foundation, "Future Labor and Skill Shortages Jeopardize American Prosperity," October 23, 2001

Since *Rewired, Rehired, or Retired?* was released in 2002, I have visited many countries and spoken to large groups of HR professionals and CEO's as well as senior management from both governmental and private enterprise organizations, covering a wide range of cultures and industries. When speaking with these people, I always ask the following questions:

- "Do you know the demographics of your workforce?"
- "Do you know what percentage of your workforce is over 50?"
- "Do you know how many of your employees will retire in the next five years?"

Consistently, only a handful of the audience (usually no more than five percent) put their hand up to indicate they know the answers to these questions. This suggests that such issues of critical concern are not high on their agenda, even for those charged with ensuring future growth and success.

I then follow up and ask:

- "Who is implementing strategies to retain and motivate your over-50 workforce?"

Whether I'm speaking with people from the United States, Brazil, Hong Kong, the United Kingdom, Australia or any other country, rarely do any hands reach for the sky.

Ask yourself:

- Do you know the answers to these questions regarding your own workforce?

If you are one of the few who may answer yes, then the follow-up question becomes:

- What strategies are you implementing to address this future challenge?

The trends and effects of the aging workforce are largely unknown, ignored, or misunderstood, and employers are refusing to put plans in place to prepare for our changing world of work.

Alarmingly, this crucial issue is not receiving the immediate required attention and does not appear to be seen as important by many organizations. Numerous human resource leaders have shared with me their attempts to discuss these issues with their CEO, where they have been met with a blank face and advised that the company has higher priorities. Short-term focus prevails!

---

Long-standing human resource practices invest heavily in youth and push out older workers. This must change—and public policy, too—or companies will find themselves running off a demographic cliff as baby boomers age.

Reprinted by permission of Harvard Business Review. From "It's Time to Retire Retirement" by K. Dychtwald, T. Erickson, and B. Morison, March 2004. Copyright © 2004 by Harvard Business School Publishing Corporation; all rights reserved.

---

Although many CEOs, HR professionals, and other members of senior management may be aware of these trends, there has not been the blueprint or mandate available to action strategies to capitalize on an aging pool of workforce talent. Today's business leaders need to address the following issues with a high degree of urgency:

- How will your organization maintain a stable, motivated, and productive workplace in step with the changing needs of your employees?
- How will your organization continue to change and respond positively to the pressures of the labor marketplace?
- How will the composition of your workforce change, and how will it affect your employment strategies?
- How will you be sure that you have sufficient workers to maximize performance next year and in five years' time?

Employers must develop ways to leverage the strengths of experienced workers and create flexible ways to motivate and retain their contributions in order to encourage them to defer or modify retirement plans. This needs to be done in an environment that also recognizes the needs and career aspirations of the diminishing pool of younger workers who will certainly not wish to see their promotion prospects stifled.

Business leaders today must immediately assess the future impact of this demographic change and adapt new strategies and policies accordingly to attract and retain their essential people power. Those CEOs who choose to keep their heads in the sand like an ostrich and focus only on short-term goals, will seal the fate for many corporations. They must act immediately to address and plan for future workplace realignment.

Keeping your head in the sand and doing nothing is NOT an option!

## Need to Work Longer

*As you go through life, you learn that if you don't paddle your own canoe, you don't move.*
Katherine Hepburn, Actress & Writer

In my mind, this is the intersection of *Rewired, Rehired, or Retired?* and this book, where both employers and employees need to 'rewire' their thinking to mitigate future risks and ensure that companies can be productive and employees can be fulfilled.

As we can see from the graph below, the number of people between the ages of 30 and 44 will actually decline between 1990 and 2025 while, at the same time, population growth for the 45–69 age group will be as high as 50 percent over the same period.

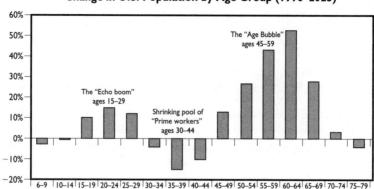

**Change in U.S. Population by Age Group (1990–2025)**

Ron Elsdon, Affiliation in the Workplace, Praeger Publishers, 2002. Reprinted with permission

While this chart reflects the dramatic change that will occur over a 35-year period in the United States, similar patterns are currently being recognized in other countries. This means we will be competing with other countries in the world (which are experiencing similar demographics) for outsourcing business and immigrants that, at a minimum, will increase the cost of these two options, making them less attractive, therefore highlighting the necessity to encourage older workers to continue working.

From the employer's point of view, there will not be enough people in the workforce to undertake job responsibilities if older workers continue to be encouraged to retire early.

However, from an older worker's perspective, because older workers are living longer, they must be sure that they have adequate savings to fund an acceptable quality of life throughout a potentially longer retirement, and therefore may need to consider postponing retirement plans to work longer, either full-time or part-time.

Across the globe there are many workers without adequate savings for retirement (if any savings at all) and have no choice but to continue working for as long as they can. Although many countries have a higher standard of living that can cushion the impact of less money in retirement via unemployment benefits and retirement pensions, these are only available when an individual reaches the specified age in which these benefits are accessible.

Populations throughout the western world are becoming increasingly aged as birthrates drop and mortality declines. It is estimated that life expectancy is currently growing at the rate of 100 days per annum. This is highlighted in Australia where, in 1975, average life expectancy was 73 years of age and by 2000 had reached 80 years. In numerous other countries, the median life expectancy is also fast approaching 80 years of age. In the United States, by the time today's 50-year-olds reach 85, their life expectancy will have increased to approximately 90. If this trend continues, a 15-year-old today can anticipate life expectancy of approximately 100 years of age.

Unlike their parents or grandparents who may have retired with little or no savings, poor health, exhausted, and with very few options following retirement, many baby boomers are arriving at mature age with the necessary vitality, wealth, and optimism to enthusiastically take on the next exciting chapter of their life with many years ahead of them.

FACT: This is the first generation of people ever to reach their 50s largely unscathed by a major war, disease, or famine.

## Mapping the Way

We are currently facing a tremendous change in the composition of our workforce in which more people are leaving than entering. The challenge now is for organizations to retain older workers to avoid employee shortages in the future. Most organizations have been slow to respond to these shifting demographics.

An important point that is often overlooked when older workers leave the workplace is that they take with them many years of experience and company history that can't be effectively replaced by new recruits coming in at the entry level. This, therefore, means possibly impacting three or four positions within the organization as people get promoted up the ranks in order to fill senior roles. Older workers are not an interchangeable component within an organization and cannot easily be replaced by outsourcing, immigration, or technology.

The world of work as we've known it has changed, and the following points and their dramatic implications must be fully understood and considered:

- The days of having "a job for life" are gone, and a new contract to replace it needs to be developed and clearly defined.
- Generation X and Generation Y workers are seeking more flexible work environments and more flexible career planning than previous generations.
- Performance management systems and career development processes must be customized. Don't assume one size fits all!
- There is a strong need to bring trust back into companies. People should be able to talk about career aspirations or concerns openly without fear of reprisal.
- A work environment and culture needs to be created where people can develop their own flexible career plan, whether it is to move up the corporate ladder, to remain stationary, or to take on fewer responsibilities and a slower pace and actually move down the corporate ladder.

- Suitable training and development programs need to be considered in relation to their desired outcome in order to avoid waste and maximize payback.
- Consideration must be given to the potential enhanced payback of taking responsibility for providing retirement planning (at least five years out) and phasing down the responsibilities for older employees.
- The importance of succession planning strategies must be recognized in order to retain and motivate potential future leaders.
- Corporate policies and environments need to be modified and adapted to meet the unique needs of our aging workforce.

If the above points are ignored, the hard truth is that organizations will face the crisis of not having enough people power to sustain future growth and will be unable to map the way to maximize opportunities for success.

The road ahead necessitates development of new initiatives and recruitment strategies. We must make certain that our organizations are sustainable in times of change so that we retain key talent who are passionate and committed to their role, resulting in supreme productivity gains, performance, and profitability.

---

*What was important yesterday may no longer be important today.*
Jack Welch, Former CEO & Chairman of General Electric

---

# In Search of Utopia

## Achieving a Winning Workplace

---

*You can't be a true idealist without being a true realist.*
Jacques Delors, French Politician & European Statesman

---

As the future looms and we are faced with the inevitable changes taking place within the workplace, we can choose to be:

(a) Ignorant—thinking it's better to focus all energies on solving today's problems;

(b) Complacent—being of the opinion that the demographic changes in the workforce won't affect your organization;

(c) Arrogant—believing you have successful workplace formulas already in place that will survive future changes; or

(d) Anticipative—to realize in advance that new policies and philosophies need to be embraced to achieve survival and ongoing success.

Of course, anticipating future changes, understanding how the responsibilities and expectations of both employer and employee will develop, and formulating and taking the steps to counter any potential negative effects are of key importance.

Our responsibility is to comprehend the big picture of the changing workplace and work towards a profitable future (and survival) by taking necessary action now. The organization of tomorrow will be significantly different from today's. However, it is possible to achieve a winning workplace, where organizations are well positioned to achieve maximum success, enjoying benefits such as the following:

- Increased productivity, performance, and profitability
- A highly motivated workforce
- Reduced staff turnover (and associated costs)
- Retention of intellectual knowledge and a successful transference of that knowledge to the next generation
- A flexible work environment
- A favored work culture that provides a competitive advantage
- Being a model employer for your industry and location
- Reduced leadership stress and sickness for high achievers
- Greater recruitment success (resulting in improved retention levels)
- Enhanced reputation in the community
- A multigenerational workforce where mutual respect is attained between generations
- Flexible career opportunities for workers of all ages
- Strong cohesive leadership team
- Retention of tomorrow's potential leaders
- Successful transition into "active" retirement (and hopefully maximizing life expectancy)

By creating an environment where individuals want to remain working on flexible terms because they are passionate and committed to their job, organizations will retain their most critical resource for the future and have greater potential to survive and prosper.

---

Best Employers understand that the key ingredient in the execution of their business strategy is the passion and commitment of their people. Highly effective leaders in these organizations work to build a differentiated culture that harnesses the power and passion of employees to deliver sustainably outstanding results for the organization.

Originally printed in Hewitt Associates Hewitt Quarterly Magazine, www.hewittasia.com. Reproduced with permission of Hewitt Associates LLC.

---

## Motivated People = Progress and Productivity

An important task for top management in the next society's corporation will be to balance the three dimensions of the corporation: as an economic organization, as a human organization and as an increasingly important social organization. Each of the three models of the corporation developed in the past half-century stressed one of these dimensions and subordinated the other two.

Obviously the enterprise can fulfill its human and social functions only if it prospers as a business. But now that knowledge workers are becoming the key employees, a company also needs to be a desirable employer to be successful.

Peter Drucker, "The Next Society, Life at the Top," November 3, 2001, *The Economist.* © 2001. The Economist Newspaper Ltd. All rights reserved. Reprinted with permission. www.economist.com

The dramatic, unprecedented period of change we are now entering means that, more than anything else, we need to address the most effective ways to retain workers. Business leaders and HR professionals must conduct the necessary research into what their employees want and endeavor to accommodate their desires for mutual benefit. As age variances within the workplace increase and job roles become modified, our role as employers and business leaders is to adapt to the changes taking place around us and understand the most effective ways to motivate and retain.

Organizations must realize their most important asset (and insurance against the crumbling of their structure) is their human component. They must recognize that implementing well-thought-out employment strategies now can determine future survival. Those who seek to achieve future success must understand the demographic changes that are occurring and offer their employees the following:

- Advancement opportunities
- Flexibility
- Respect for each individual's talents, regardless of age
- Competitive compensation
- Recognition and feedback for achievements
- Education and support relating to change
- Ongoing training and development for workers of all ages
- Opportunities to learn from more experienced workers or workers with different skills

- Respect for lifestyle requirements and work/life balance
- Open communication regarding change, progress, concerns, goals, and market expectations
- Performance optimization
- Clear communication of future opportunities
- Succession planning
- Opportunity to phase down to fewer responsibilities
- Empowerment to take control of their own careers
- Alignment of corporate and individual goals

According to "The Future of Work Survey," conducted by DBM in 2003, "Lifestyle" will become the dominant issue for employees in 2013: "Lifestyle replaces security and compensation as the clear number one issue of the future for employees."

---

Ric Charlesworth coached the Australian women's hockey team, the Hockeyroos, to back-to-back gold medals at the Atlanta and Sydney Olympics, and managed to keep them at the top of the international ladder for eight years.

He says the two basic coaching differences between sport and business are lack of imperative and lack of frequent and precise measurement in the latter.

"In business, it is possible to make profits and grow without being the best. It is possible to be comfortable in the middle of the pack," he says. "Rarely would a sporting team be deemed successful without winning the premiership, gold medal or championship."

Charlesworth believes that very often the difference between rival teams and companies isn't the quality of the game plan, but its execution.

He has a five-step formula for building through teamwork "a resilient group capable of handling any threat from any foe"—a team with a margin for error to overcome the vagaries of competition at the highest level:

- **Quality**—values, people and practices. "The core values of the group or organization underpin how you go about your business," so time spent in selecting those values is fundamental. Choosing quality people demands that you truly know them, or get to know them, before the selection is confirmed.
- **Teamwork**—you have to work at it. "Tolerance, sharing, selflessness and thinking about others aren't always the most natural inclinations. The skill of the coach and the manager is in bal-

ancing a sometimes contradictory set of values—individual competitive zeal and team goals."

- **Training**—excellence is not an act but a habit. Sport, much like business, is a chaotic drama in which performers and spectators do not know what will happen next. Charlesworth's coaching habit is to overload training with decisions and complexity in order to develop athletes who can handle a lot of information and make decisions in an environment of hot competition and fatigue.
- **Resilience**—springing back to action. Something that is resilient will spring back into shape after it has been bent or distorted by some outside force. Charlesworth says the capacity to put things in perspective after adversity and move on is crucial in sport and business.
- **Depth and flexibility**—the many uncontrollable variables in sport and business deliver constant change. Charlesworth, six-time winner of the Australian Coach of the Year award, says the best preparation for sudden change is to practice adapting to change. He does this by requiring players to play unfamiliar positions in training and in games, and by emphasizing the need to multiskill every player.

Once a team or an individual has achieved success—winning the premiership or a gold medal, or achieved the pinnacle of market share and/or profitability, it is human nature to relax and enjoy the experiences, praise and high altitude. Vigilance and a strategy for staying on top are equally important once you get there," says Charlesworth. "Indeed, while achieving success you should be putting in place practices that will ensure continued success once you are there."

Charlesworth offers five principles for remaining the best team in sport and business:

- **Continue with the core principles.** Most successful organizations and teams reach the stage where they forget what it was that made them great.
- **Redefine the challenges.** Charlesworth quotes other top coaches in saying:

    "Challenges once met are no longer challenges. The challenge itself must be enriched or renewed periodically."

    "In the workplace, it is often those who are comfortable and feel able to do their job without much hassle who need to be challenged with new tasks, new demands and new requests."
- **Refresh the team.** Just as individuals need to be renewed and refreshed by new challenges, so does your team. According to Charlesworth, nothing refreshes a team more than the introduction of new talent and new faces.

- **Avoid recycling.** One of the most seductive tendencies for the successful organization is to keep doing things the same way. After all, the methods are proved and achieved results last time. Charlesworth vehemently warns against the sporting dictum "Never change a winning team." Instead, he actively seeks to deliberately develop and introduce new ideas and methods into each component of a team, whether winning or losing.
- **Face your foes.** Once you start to lose awareness of the practices that underpin your success, performance and consistency diminish. "There is a little voice inside you that tells you it is someone else's turn. This is arrant nonsense. It is never anyone's turn to win the gold medal at the Olympics; it must be earned," Charlesworth says.

  Another dangerous complacency-based foe is the expectation that "it'll be okay on the day." Charlesworth warns: "Because in the past things have worked on the day we think that it will be the same again."

John Lyons, "Mind over Muscle," *The Australian Financial Review*, September 3, 2002

---

## Success Strategies

Obviously, organizations' principles and goals differ greatly throughout the world. But, by taking a look at some examples of those who have taken (or are taking) the necessary steps to meet the challenges of tomorrow head-on, we can gain some valuable tips for future survival.

The organizations in the case studies featured below are at various stages of addressing issues regarding the imminent labor crisis. Some are well on their way to ensuring a successful future, whereas some still have a lot of work to do. Perhaps you will identify with one or more of these organizations and be inspired by their proactive approach.

It should be noted that I am a director of two of the organizations featured, Coates Hire and Cordukes Limited. When researching relevant case studies, I realized these two examples were right under my nose. Both Coates Hire and Cordukes Limited are endeavoring to become employers of choice, and they have successfully implemented many of the suggestions outlined in this book.

The following examples detail a diverse range of companies who, although they are at various stages of change implementation, share the view that embracing change and developing the necessary effective strategies for future survival and success is an ongoing journey.

**Case Study 1**

Organization:  British Telecom (BT)
Industry:   Telecommunications
Country:   United Kingdom
No. of employees: 105,000
No. of customers: 21 million

BT is currently striving to become the ultimate employer of choice and, in 2002, they were named Employer of the Year by the U.K. Department of Trade and Industry. When focusing on recruiting young people that year, BT had 15,000 applicants for 400 graduate positions (usually receiving approximately 10,000 applicants for these positions each year), proving that BT is an organization that young people want to join. Their retention rate is one to be proud of—staff turnover is only 3 percent.

BT is proud that they don't discriminate against their older workers (19 percent of their staff is over 50). In fact, full training opportunities are made available and workers can continue working beyond the usual retirement age of 60 if they choose. BT is committed to looking after their older contingent both before and after retirement. Prior to retirement, loved ones are invited to be included in planning sessions for life beyond the retirement date. Many workers who have retired from BT willingly become re-employed during peak times, enabling BT to access their wealth of experience on a casual and reliable basis. They have 180,000 pensioners, many of whom remain actively involved with the organization.

During the late 1990s, BT decided to recruit to align with the diversity of their customer base, and therefore employed many workers in their 40s and 50s in particular, as well as people from diverse ethnic backgrounds. BT believes in recruiting from the widest talent pool possible.

BT respects the individual needs of their workers and have adopted many policies to ensure workplace fulfillment, including their New Start program, which features the following:

- "Step Down"—which enables people to step down to less responsibility and work part-time if they choose. They have a 97 percent success rate of complying with people's requests.

1.5 percent find a compromise and only 1.5 percent are denied their request.

- "Helping Hands"—where employees can undertake a sabbatical for an agreed period of time, often to assist a charity.
- Flexibility—70,000 of their total 105,000 employees work flexible hours, with 8,500 people working from home.
- "Deployment"—where work is distributed out to people to complete in teams.
- "Student Placement Service"—where university students can undertake paid work with BT during their holidays for three to four months as well as working on special assignments. This has proven to be a successful prerecruitment strategy where those that perform well are offered employment at the end of their studies.
- "Healthy Lifestyle Programs"—providing education about maintaining health for a healthier workforce.

Although the company has undertaken significant downsizing over the past ten years (they have let go 160,000 people), there has been no loss of work time due to industrial unrest. Employees generally understand the reality of work and believe the company is doing the best they can for their employees.

Caroline Waters, BT Group's Director People Networks, believes BT is truly an employer of choice and that their investments today will create the right culture for tomorrow. She says, "From the moment they first join the organization, all employees of BT are encouraged to create their life plan and ensure they have the proper balance between life at work and outside work. These plans are regularly revisited and reviewed with supervisors to ensure employees are on track and are professionally and personally fulfilled, which therefore translates into improved productivity and profitability."

---

*Since WWII, the economy has grown 8-fold while the labor force has only grown 2–2.5 times. This means that the average worker is about four times as productive now as they were in 1946.*
Allan Scheweyer, Senior Analyst, HR.com

---

## Case Study 2

| | |
|---|---|
| Organization: | Thomson Learning, A Division of the Thomson Corporation |
| Industry: | Education and Training |
| Country: | United States |
| No. of employees: | 12,000 worldwide |

Thomson Learning is a great example of a forward thinking, flexible employer who has conducted the necessary research to understand how the dynamics of their workforce will change over the next ten years, and they are now making the necessary preparations.

Their workforce is progressively aging and they are addressing the important changes that must be made in order to retain their aging members for as long as possible. In fact, Thomson Learning has recently assisted some of their senior executives to phase down from their full-time roles into part-time roles. This has enabled these people to achieve the work/life balance they desire while, at the same time, allowing Thomson Learning to retain these valuable contributors.

In order to attract and retain younger workers, Thomson Learning has introduced a number of programs that are proving successful, such as the following:

- Education assistance programs to undertake further study, including financial support and time off to attend lectures
- Flexible work hours
- Provision of summer hours (work hard for four days per week and have three-day weekends)
- Half-day Fridays
- Attractive and competitive pay
- A stimulating learning environment
- Leadership Development Programs
- Offering stock options to high potentials
- Open communication of financial results
- Regular performance reviews conducted with supervisors
- Regular engagement reviews (climate surveys) and acting upon them
- An MBA program and other ongoing training opportunities
- Providing a winning workplace culture that employees are proud to be a part of

Thomson Learning's philosophy is to encourage all people to reach their full potential through strategies such as the following:

- The "Pathway to Prime" program, where key people meet to discuss and implement ways to improve the organization and are empowered to do so
- Making sure that good people stay with the organization, even if their particular department is being downsized or sold. This is by way of identifying other suitable roles for them within the Thomson Corporation and offering "stay" incentives.
- Advertising available positions within the group and encouraging existing staff to apply
- Offering promotional opportunities. 65 percent of senior appointments are made from internal applicants
- A very dynamic performance management system
- Creating a culture where employees can express their views openly
- Striving to align corporate and personal goals and clear goal setting for development
- Maintaining an environment of trust
- Offering incentive schemes
- Reviewing each person's role within Thomson Learning to identify the person's contribution and future potential. (Two days per year are dedicated to this by senior management of the Thomson Corporation, including the CEO.)

In the words of Thomson Learning's Sr. Vice President for Human Resources, Steve Mower, "Motivation is a result, not a process." He says, "People who work with Thomson Learning believe they can grow within the company and are offered performance based remuneration and incentives. Thomson Learning is constantly reviewing productivity and changes required to prepare for the future."

---

High and needless turnover is a bad thing. It's expensive and it's noticed—by your remaining employees, by your competitors, and, if you do nothing to reverse the trend, by your customers. Former secretary of labor, Robert Reich, talks about a test he gives to employees he meets in his travels during lecture tours. He asks, "What do you do here?" The employee answers one of two ways: "I operate a word processor in the legal department" or "We process legal documents to assist other departments in servicing our customers." The manner in which the employee answers tells Reich a lot about the company the employee works for, and about how the individual regards that company. In organizations with high levels of retention, the "we" pronoun is heard more frequently.

Maureen Sullivan, *The Gen-Xer Guide to Boomerangers*, DBM Publishing, New York, p. 91

## Case Study 3

Organization:      Coates Hire
Industry:           Equipment Hire
Country:            Australia
No. of employees:  1,900

Coates Hire is an organization that understands the true worth of their workforce and recently won a "Champion of the Mature Worker" award from the Australian government in recognition of their positive approach to their aging workforce. They have a number of initiatives in place to increase staff loyalty and retention, which are proving to be very successful, including the following:

- No enforced retirement date
- Encouraging workers to keep working. (Their oldest employee is 72.)
- Offering Leadership development programs for talented staff
- Increasing training opportunities for workers at all levels and ages, without discrimination
- Five weeks' annual leave (when industry requirement is four weeks)
- Employee share program (92 percent participation)
- Offering income protection
- Regular reward and recognition for achievements
- Believing in open communication at all levels to build trust
- Growth development strategies
- Management succession plan
- Working towards aligning personal and corporate goals
- Regular communication of the organization's results so that employees can share the vision
- Conducting climate surveys to understand employee's views with uncensored feedback
- Identifying clear links between high morale of staff and profits

15 percent of Coates Hire's total workforce is over 51, and these older workers are well respected by the younger workers.

Workers of all ages mix successfully to create an extremely productive environment. The organization is striving to empower employees to feel more in control of their own careers. The fact that 92 percent of employees are shareholders in the company means it's not just a job for them.

Due to the geographic spread of Coates Hire's 150 branches throughout Australia, recruiting young apprentices straight from school has proved difficult because not all young people want to remain in regional areas. In order to overcome these workforce shortages, Coates Hire has offered apprenticeships to workers in their 20s and 30s who are willing to learn new skills and develop their career within the organization.

Malcolm Jackman, CEO of Coates Hire, has a strong HR background and respects the people he works with and the influence they have over the future of the company. He regularly visits Coates Hire offices to speak personally with all staff members, and he likes to wear the standard blue cotton Coates Hire shirt to demonstrate he's part of the team. He encourages an open door policy where employees feel they can speak to him directly, and he makes a point of sending personalized Christmas cards to all employees.

Jackman doesn't believe in the term "employer of choice" as he believes it should be more about the workplace as a whole rather than the employer. He prefers to use the expression "a place where employees want to work" and credits the positive turnaround experienced by Coates Hire as "victories are making it happen and success breeds success."

---

*Watch the turtle. He only moves forward by sticking his neck out.*
Louis Gerstner, Former CEO & Chairman of IBM

---

## Case Study 4

| | |
|---|---|
| Organization: | Cordukes Limited |
| Industry: | Building & Construction/Asset & Facilities Management |
| Country: | Australia |
| No. of employees: | 650 |

Cordukes Limited has recently gone through an enormous amount of change after recording significant losses. Although it is only two years into their turnaround, it is evident the strategies they now have in place are taking a positive effect by improved profits. These strategies include the following:

- Implementing performance management systems
- No age bias
- Introducing flexibility to work hours when required
- Providing challenging tasks and treating people well
- Employee share program (65 percent participation)
- Upgrading premises to a more attractive, modern environment
- Morale boosting days with special staff events
- Recognizing achievements at local branch level
- Communicating values to all staff
- Encouraging a sense of community
- Creating a sense of pride
- Commitment to personal growth and development and creating an environment of trust
- Leadership training
- Advancement opportunities for those performing well

This is the Cordukes Limited value statement:

---

At Cordukes Limited, we value integrity and we display this by doing what we say, and always being honest, sincere and fair.

We value our people including our relationships with customers and suppliers. We provide our people with a safe environment where learning and self-fulfillment are integral to the way we work.

Finally, we undertake all activities with ownership and accountability. We proudly represent our company and always strive to add value to our customers.

---

Cordukes Limited believes in the philosophy that people can continue working within their organization no matter what their age, as long as they keep performing. Workers of all ages work successfully together within the group.

Since Martin Whittaker, the CEO of Cordukes Limited, was appointed in 2002, he has successfully transformed the company from an environment of fear to an environment of trust. He believes in respecting each person's worth and dignity and understands the importance of treating people well, not just from a corporate retention perspective, but also so that individuals are empowered and confident to lead their lives. Earlier in Whittaker's career, he experienced firsthand what it was like to be given an unforseen, humiliating departure and vows never to treat anyone with disrespect.

Whittaker believes there is still a lot of work to do before they can claim the title of employer of choice, however, with the strategies now being implemented, they are now well on their way. He says that "becoming an employer of choice is an achievement that a company earns through the consistent application of sound people-management practices. Such consistent application creates an environment in which employees want to come to work and give their best because their key needs are met."

Whittaker recently shared the following "employer of choice" information with his management team to ensure clarity of the organization's aspirations:

"Employer of choice" organizations:
- Create a work environment that is innovative and challenging, in the pursuit of competitive business success;
- Let all employees know what is expected of them, how they are progressing, and what they need to do to improve yet further;
- Communicate frequently and candidly with employees about the business;
- Provide employees with the information, training, equipment and materials they need to do their job;
- Ensure employees receive recognition and reward for good work;
- Encourage the continuous professional development and growth of all employees;
- Value and encourage all employees' opinions;
- Ensure that each employee knows that he/she is cared about and respected as a person;
- Are clear about their values (quality, accountability, integrity, teamwork and learning) and work consistently and actively to make them the prevailing culture; and
- Recognize the employee stakeholder as a source of competitive advantage in delivering shareholders' expectations.

Being an employer of choice does not mean paying the most. It does not mean things are soft and undisciplined with the company. Rather, it means paying employees a competitive rate for their contribution, being fair and insisting that good business standards are effectively implemented. It is about maintaining personal accountability by every individual for high performance and learning.

You know you are an employer of choice when:

- High-quality people approach the company for career opportunities;
- Employees recommend their employer to friends and associates;
- Employees live the values of the company, understanding that they have an important stake in its future; and
- Employees willingly give of their discretionary efforts to contribute to the achievement of outstanding business results (because it is something that is important to them).

---

*Winning isn't everything, but wanting to win is.*
Vince Lombardi, Football Coach

---

## Case Study 5

Organization: Foxtel/Austar
Industry: Entertainment
Country: Australia
No. of employees: 2,500 people (employs an additional 1,000 on a contractual basis)

Since commencing services in 1995, Foxtel/Austar has enjoyed dramatic success and is Australia's leading subscription television provider. Upon entering their Sydney premises, you immediately become impressed by the positive, dynamic, and vibrant environment and the fact that everyone is smiling.

Foxtel/Austar has experienced a high turnover due to the many opportunities currently available to transfer skills within the television industry in Australia and other countries. Although it is company policy to promote from within whenever possible, opportunities are not always available for those wanting to develop their careers.

Their philosophy is to provide ongoing training to all employees, no matter what their age, although the majority of their employees tend to be under 45 due to the highly evolving television industry. Those who are over 45 are definitely young at heart.

When seeking new recruits, their number one goal (providing they have the required skills) is to employ to fit the culture. They have no problem employing a 60-year-old who possesses the right attitude and skills over a 25-year-old with the right skills but wrong attitude.

Foxtel/Austar strives to retain good people by providing them with the following:

- A commitment to their development
- Regular training opportunities
- Flexible working hours
- A creative environment
- State-of-the-art technology
- Rehirement opportunities when required
- Recognition and rewards for achievements
- Free Foxtel/Austar cable television connection
- Pride in their working environment
- Regular opportunities to have views heard, via climate surveys and team meetings
- A shared vision
- Empowerment and support to control their own careers

Cherie Romaro, General Manager of Foxtel/Austar's Arena & Weather Television Channels in Australia, believes in the importance of flexibility in the workplace. She says, "Family is important, and if someone requires time we endeavour to accommodate their individual requirements. With many young parents working here, babies and children are regulars in the office. Balance is key and we find that by providing individuals with the flexibility they need to achieve their work/life balance, they are more than willing to put in the extra hours when under pressure to deliver."

---

*Managing creative people is an oxymoron. You don't manage them at all. Instead you provide an environment in which they can be simultaneously stimulated and protected, challenged and encouraged, exposed and private.* Nicholas Negroponte, Professor of Media Technology, Massachusetts Institute of Technology

---

## The Perfect World

We may not all believe in the possibility of a perfect world or utopia, but there's no reason why we shouldn't all be searching and striving for it. We can learn from the experience of others (and our own mistakes) and confront future realities swiftly and honestly, in order to be fully prepared to deal with the impending changes to our workforce.

The brutal reality is that successful companies in the next five years will be those who have addressed these issues and have adopted a flexible workplace structure to retain and motivate their multigenerational workforce, a workforce who has different aspirations from any workforce of the past.

Having the courage to face the facts and implement new strategies to arm against future negative forces will give you the best opportunity to achieve a profitable future.

---

The restructuring effort proved to be a crucial element in creating the streamlined GE that Welch knew was needed. But Jack Welch sensed that it was not enough, and that to create a truly agile, competitive enterprise required more—much more.

To transform GE into a world-class company, he would have to devise a new strategy. A strategy capable of supercharging an arguably weakened workforce. The downsizing of the 1980s had reduced the number of GE employees by almost a third, and those still standing were reeling, consumed by worry for their own jobs. After all, they wondered, if GE could simply snap their fingers and eliminate all those jobs, what's to stop them from cutting mine next?

Welch recognized the problem, and he knew that he needed to give GE employees—the survivors—a sense of how to behave in the new, lean environment. He would have to do something that would help diminish the uneasiness and rebuild confidence and self-worth.

He summed up his prescription for winning in three words:

- Speed (Speed decreases control)
- Simplicity (Simple enough for cocktail party chatter)
- Self-Confidence (The antidote to insecurity)

"If you don't have self-confidence," says Welch, "you can't be simple. You just can't. You're scared to death that you'll look simple. The way to sabotage your chances of producing great bottom-line results is to bog the organization down in complicated, distracting clutter. The surest path to failure is to create the kinds of bureaucratic sloth and sluggishness that slow your business down."

But, a business leader asks, justifiably, How can I avoid all these things—the monitoring, the checking, the approvals? We've been doing these things for years. And they seem to work.

Welch's answer is, not surprisingly, a simple one: Have the self-confidence to make meaningful changes in your business. Have the self-confidence to simplify and speed up your business procedures. Speed, simplicity, and self-confidence may sound like dozens of other business aphorisms. But when they are truly encouraged and developed, they are powerful management tools that can help streamline your organization and boost the productivity of your entire workforce. It's really as simple as that.

Robert Slater, Jack Welch and the GE Way, McGraw Hill. Copyright © 1989. This material is reproduced with the permission of the McGraw Hill Companies.

# 3

# Recycle Old Perceptions

## A Rolling Stone Gathers No Moss

---

Mick Jagger in his 20s was quoted as saying that his greatest night-
mare was that he and the Rolling Stones would still be singing "Satisfaction" by the time he turned 40 and that he intended to retire
before middle age for fear that the Rolling Stones might become
an anachronistic parody of themselves.

---

$B$ack in the 1960s a favorite mantra of the time was "never trust
anyone over 30." There was a perception that those over 30
weren't in touch with current developments and that future
progress depended on the energetic youth of the day. Oh, how
history repeats itself! It was only recently that we had the dot-com
boom where the young guns dominated and believed those over
30 were no longer relevant. Older workers were deemed useless
throughout the dot-com boom, however, they sure had what it
took to rebuild, restructure, and revive the ruins of the dot-com
"bust."

Michael Philip Jagger was a shy, middle-class student at the
London School of Economics studying for his Bachelor of Economics degree back in the 60s. Foolishly, he was sidetracked and
decided to focus his energies on forming a rock band. He with-
drew from his studies (a fear most parents dread) and rapidly
gained a reputation as someone who offended and outraged the
older generation.

Now, if Mick had stayed and completed his economics degree,
he may have joined a corporation or perhaps the government as
a public servant and, if diligent, hardworking, and loyal, would
have gradually been promoted up the ranks of the organization.

Mick turned 60 on July 26, 2003. If he had been employed in
the corporate world, there's a very good chance he may have been

laid off in the last wave of downsizings, lined up to be included in the next round of "rightsizings," or pushed out of the organization altogether. His employer may have deemed him to be "past it" and told him it was time to phase down and consider retirement.

Instead, Mick and the Rolling Stones are still recording albums and undertake regular high-grossing tours around the globe with energy and enthusiasm. In fact, since 1989, the Stones have grossed $1.5 billion. Now Mick Jagger (or Sir Michael Jagger if you prefer) can reflect on a full and successful life where he has followed his passions, continues to work hard and *"Not Fade Away."* It wouldn't surprise me if loyal (and ageless) Rolling Stones fans were still lining up in ten years' time to purchase tickets to their concerts.

We have to ask ourselves why Mick Jagger is still considered to "have it" in one industry, yet, in the corporate world, Mick Jagger may be seen to be "past it" with regard to his usefulness in an organization in the business world.

## Longer Life

*We are in the grandest social experiment ever witnessed by humankind: in the last 90 years longevity in western culture has increased 30 years!*
"The New Retirement," Richard Johnson, RetirementOptions.com

I recently entered the word *aging* into my computer's thesaurus. As someone who is considered a member of the aging workforce, I was horrified to see words like *shriveled, declining, foolish, decrepit, deteriorated* and even *senile, driveling, doddering, ugly, moribund* and *dying*!

I foolishly then entered the word *young* and was presented with words such as *strength, hopeful, in-touch, developing, productive, ageless, healthy, fresh* and *vigorous*. Sure, we may have a few more wrinkles and gray hairs, but I'd like to think that we experienced workers possess the majority of these so-called youthful qualities too.

In many countries today, people enjoy better health than at any other time, possess greater financial resources, and have broader retirement options, including the choice to retire at a later age or, at least in the traditional sense of retirement, not at all. We are now redefining aging as we know it.

Our perception of what we classify as old age varies around the world. What seemed an old age 20 or 30 years ago is no longer the situation. Being "old" at 40 or 50 is ridiculous, particularly when we examine the growth in life expectancy today in most countries.

---

*Demography is destiny.*
Auguste Comte, French Philosopher

---

Advances in medicine and health practices have helped double the average life span of Americans in the past 200 years (Butler, 2000). So, with the average life expectancy today in many countries approaching approximately 80 years of age, someone who's 50 today can expect to see the average life expectancy rise to 90 when the person is 85. In other words, over the next 35 years, life expectancy will grow by 10 years.

Because time is no longer a scarce resource, older individuals considering their future must now rethink their retirement plans and recognize the need to work longer to be certain that they have adequate savings to fund the quality of life they desire.

In light of current trends, we need to revisit the old thinking that prevails and look for new perspectives on how to leverage the powerful knowledge and experience of older workers. Employers must now appreciate and enhance what these workers can offer to ensure they are well prepared for the long term.

## Why 65?

---

*Age is whatever you think it is. You are as old as you think you are.*
Muhammad Ali, World Champion Heavyweight Boxer

---

So who defines when we're "past it"? For so long now, 65 has represented the maximum age where you say good-bye to your coworkers and retire into a life of leisure (and often boredom). For some reason there's a view that at 64 years and 11 months you are "useful" and at 65 years and one month you are "useless." Why does such a short time frame have such impact? It's crazy to think a person is no longer capable of making a quality contribution to your organization just because of his or her age.

In fact, the age of 65 was originally made the age of retirement back in the late nineteenth century by a Prussian general named Otto Von Bismarck. Bismarck generously made available a retirement benefit to those soldiers who made it to the age of 65. (In those days the average life expectancy was 45.) Approximately 10 percent of his army actually lived to collect their benefits – not exactly the safest job around! This is tantamount to our governments today announcing "Good news for retirees. The retirement pensions are going to be increased fourfold, however, you'll have to wait until you're 85 to receive any of the benefits."

It's hard to accept that this outdated precedent of 65 being the magic, maximum age to retire has any basis on deciding who should and shouldn't be working in our organizations today. With improved health and life expectancy, a retirement age that was decided well over 100 years ago is hardly relevant now. We've been stuck in a groove, and it's time to make decisions based on reality, rather than accepting a tired, old manifesto.

Recently the American government announced that those people under 41 would have to wait until they are 67 before getting retirement benefits. This is only a small adjustment when we consider how life expectancy has grown dramatically since the days of General Von Bismarck.

While mandatory ages for retirement are disappearing in many countries, many employers are still strongly encouraging their 50+ workers to take early retirement.

## Myths of Old

Sadly, many organizations aren't embracing the talents and contributions of the older members of their workforce due to discriminatory misperceptions and ignorance regarding their long-term validity. Successful companies of tomorrow must overcome the numerous myths relating to experienced workers, including that older workers:

- Are more rigid, less open-minded, and set in their ways.
- View new ideas in a negative manner and prefer to focus on what might go wrong instead of focusing on a more effective way to achieve a goal that will save money, time, and effort.
- Have preconceived ideas and prefer to write a conclusion before researching and attempting the task.

- Are risk-adverse, suspicious of change, and will always take the most conservative view without assessing the risk/reward equation.
- Are fearful of new technology and don't wish to continue learning.
- Look to the past rather than the future for inspiration and rely on past experiences rather than exploring new methods.
- Procrastinate too much and are always sick and complaining.
- Want to be rewarded for loyalty rather than performance.
- Are less effective on the job than a younger person is.

In fairness, there are some workers in the baby boomer and mature worker categories who do fit the stereotype as described above and unfortunately exacerbate these misconceptions. Fortunately, they are in the minority.

What do we really know, and what do we think we know about the career myths and realities confronting older workers today? In many parts of the world, there is a commonly held belief that older workers are likely to react differently to certain situations in the work environment than their younger colleagues. And, let's be clear about it, the implication lurking behind this view is that the older worker is going to be more rigid and less open-minded, risk-adverse, and suspicious of change, or that they will look to the past, not the future, for inspiration.

But how difficult, conceptually at least, is it to take that view and stand it on its head? What if we argue that by virtue of their ability to combine years of real-world experience with a life-long sense of practical and intellectual curiosity, older workers actually bring more to the business table: a more valuable view of future opportunities grounded in hard-learned lessons from the past?

You don't need to look far for examples to support either point of view. During the dot-com craze of the late 1990s, for instance, people could (and probably did) tell you that anyone over the age of 40 (or was it 30, or even 20?) could simply not be part of this phenomenon and, by implication, was excluded from the future of business. If you wanted proof, you had only to look at stock valuations and the riches generated by initial public offerings. Youth ruled.

Then, in 2000, when many of these stock prices imploded, people could (and probably did) tell you that, on second thought, it probably would have made sense for those companies to have retained the experience of individuals who had actually developed a new product or created a new service at some point in their careers. Experience ruled.

The world's largest organization of older people, the AARP, with more than 30 million members, surveyed employers' attitudes toward older workers. Older workers received ratings of "excellent" or "very good" on the following qualities. (The percentages indicate the proportion of employers in the survey who gave these ratings.)

- Attendance and punctuality, 86 percent
- Commitment to quality, 82 percent
- Loyalty to employer, 79 percent
- Practical knowledge, 79 percent
- Solid experience, 74 percent
- Reliable performance, 74 percent

What is clear is that many of the myths can be dispelled, and it comes down to the attitude and capabilities of the employee, whether young or old, as to their ability to perform efficiently.

Despite age discrimination laws in most countries, many people over 40 often find it difficult to get an interview with a recruitment firm (and it seems to get progressively worse the older you are). This is usually because of outdated beliefs, either from the recruitment consultants or the organization they are representing, based on the many myths relating to older workers that still exist.

---

Despite the warnings, employers are unprepared for the aging workforce and the labor squeeze. A study of 1,104 workers aged over 45 in three federal agencies found management was out of touch with the views of their older staff and also underestimated their commitment.

The Federal Minister for Aging, Kevin Andrews, is developing a national strategy for an aging Australia and is also involved in creating the nation's first age discrimination bill. "I think unfortunately it's the culture amongst those who are doing the hiring and firing," he said. "Quite often they are young themselves. Maybe a start is having HR managers who are 45 to 50. They should have a cross-section of people who are doing the hiring. It might change the culture considerably."

"Looming Labor Crisis Puts the Focus on Gray Force," by Sherrill Nixon, *Sydney Morning Herald*, October 2, 2002

---

## Age Busters

---

*"Youth is not entirely a time of life: It is a state of mind.*

*It is not wholly a matter of ripe cheeks. It is a temper of the will, a quality of the imagination, vigor of the emotions, a freshness of the deep springs of life.*

*It means a temperamental predominance of courage over timidity, of an appetite for adventure over love of ease.*

*Nobody grows old by merely living a number of years.*

*People grow old only by deserting their ideals.*

*Years may wrinkle the skin, but to give up interest, wrinkles the soul.*

*Worry, doubt, self-distrust, fear, and despair—are the long, long years that bow the head and turn the growing spirit back to dust.*

*In the central place of every heart there is a recording chamber; so long as it receives messages of beauty, hope, cheer, and courage—so long are you young.*

*When the wires are all down and your heart is covered with the snows of pessimism and the ice of cynicism—then, and then only, are you grown old."*
General Douglas MacArthur on his 75th birthday

---

Thankfully, there is a multitude of mature individuals throughout the world who defy the concept of "being too old." Take, for example, the head of the Federal Reserve Bank, Alan Greenspan, undoubtedly one of the most powerful people in the United States. In 2003 the President offered Greenspan, then 77, a further four-year contract, as he is valued as too important to retire (and there was obviously no succession plan in place). In fact, back in 1980, 70-year-old Ronald Reagan was elected President, yet he would have probably been too old to get a job in most companies.

Consider Peter Drucker, possibly the greatest economist and business writer of the past 50 years, born in 1909 and still going strong and producing great work. There's John Glenn who went into space at age 77 and Sir Francis Chichester who completed the first solo circumnavigation with only one stop at the age of 67. Barbara Cartland was still writing novels at 96, and Mother Theresa worked tirelessly until she died at 87.

Other "age busters," just to name a few, who have no intention of slowing down (at the time of writing) include Warren Buffet (73), Rupert Murdoch (72), Madeleine Albright (66), Willie Nelson (70) and Queen Elizabeth (77). Nelson Mandela was 76 when he became President of South Africa and remains an inspirational leader internationally.

A number of older movie stars are still going strong, such as Sean Connery, Gene Hackman, Paul Newman, Michael Caine, Dame Judy Dench, James Garner, Lauren Bacall, Maggie Smith, and Clint Eastwood (who is still chasing villains well into his 70s).

Recently, while visiting Toronto, I heard about Hazel McCallion. At 82, Hazel is the longest serving Mayor of Missasauga, Ontario. Apparently, Hazel has ruled with an iron-fisted, no-nonsense approach and has always been reelected unopposed over the past 16 years. It seems Hazel is regarded as single-handedly being responsible for making Missasauga the go-ahead, dynamic city it is today and has developed a successful corporate environment with many new business centers being established. The city has not had to borrow money since 1978 and is currently debt-free and has kept taxes low for over a decade. She has played a leading role for women's politics and has a list of credits a mile long. Although Hazel McCallion has a mayoral limousine available to her, she refuses to use it and always prefers to drive herself around in her own car. Hazel has no plans to retire.

Asked which of his works he would select as his masterpiece, architect Frank Lloyd Wright at 83 replied, "my next one."

# 4

# Age of Reasoning

## Baby Boomers

In the U.S. today, someone turns 50 every eight seconds—that's 11,000 per day. By 2006 nearly 80 million aging baby boomers will total a little less than one-third of the nation's population. In the 20-year period from 2010 to 2030 the portion of the U.S. population over age 65 is expected to grow by as much as it had grown in the prior 80 years.

*Demographics & Destiny: Winning the War for Talent.* © 2004 Watson Wyatt Worldwide. All rights reserved.

In countries such as the United States, Canada, Australia, and the United Kingdom, a huge population growth (the baby boom) was experienced from the period following WWII up until the early 1960s when the pill was introduced. Never before had we experienced such high fertility rates. According to AARP, baby boomers represent the largest single sustained growth of the population in the history of the United States.

Baby boomers, those born between 1946 and 1964, are showing no signs of slowing down. In the next 20 years, as the Boomers age, "oldies" will outnumber children for the first time.

Many new industries are now marketed at baby boomers (or "young elders"), such as the numerous websites, magazines, and associations such as AARP as well as specific employment and travel agencies that appeal to the active boomer, not to mention the plethora of antiaging treatments and cure-alls that are now available.

Baby Boomers. It is an unlikely innocent term for the most powerful social group of the age. Those two words suggest comfortable domesticity and parenthood, but the Baby Boom generation is a great deal more—it is challenging, exciting and dangerous.

This generation represents the biggest spending, best-educated and most sophisticated group of consumers in history. The first of this generation, the ones who entered a world of Dinky Toys, Listen With Mother and short trousers half a century ago, are now well advanced in the business of taking over the reins of power for themselves. Famously, President Bill Clinton is a boomer. So, too, are Bill Gates, Oprah Winfrey, and Steven Spielberg.

"Boom On," Mike Durham, *Viewpoint Magazine*, Netherlands

The baby boomer generation is, however, inevitably aging and will become eligible for retirement between now and 2029. Many boomers are opting to work longer to fund their retirement and maintain the quality of life they have grown used to. Those who opt to retire early at, for example, 55 must plan how their savings will last for the next 35 years or so to make sure that they have a quality existence. A number of boomers have the added financial hindrance of caring for children and, sometimes, grandchildren who continue to live at home, as well as dependant elderly parents (which is becoming more of a common occurrence).

The baby boomers are the largest-growing segment of the workforce today, and from a social, medical, economic, and political point of view, the world economies are ill prepared for this evolving trend.

## The Age Bubble

The Age Bubble is the balloon effect created by the baby boomers whenever they do something en masse. Because of their large numbers, their impact has been felt at every stage of their lives. For example:

- Overcrowded maternity wards in hospitals.
- Starting school and consequently college, which led to overcrowded classrooms, the demand for more teachers, and a building boom in new schools and colleges.
- When they were children they outnumbered the 65+ generation (in some countries four to one).
- Embracing rock'n'roll as their own culture through groups such as the Beatles and the Rolling Stones.
- Increased demand for housing.
- Entering the workforce.
- Having children.
- Turning 50.

As the leading edge of the baby boom generation prepares for retirement, about one-third of the boomers surveyed are planning to keep on working. In addition, about one-third is considering more education and about two-thirds consider traveling and volunteering as important.

"Our study suggests that there is a fundamental shift in how baby boomers view retirement," comments Phyllis Moen, a professor of sociology and human development at Cornell. "Overall, we find that the baby boomers are retiring in a society where the economy, gender roles, families, and retirement itself are in a state of flux. Old cultural norms and institutional policies regarding retirement are out of date. Communities, workplaces, and society will have to accommodate aging baby boomers who will move into retirement healthier, better educated and more energetic than any previous generation and who don't want their fathers' retirement," says Moen. "I anticipate that baby boomers will transform the very meaning of retirement, as they have transformed institutions and expectations as this remarkably large group moved through kindergarten, college, early adulthood, and midlife."

Cornell University, "A Third of Baby Boomers Plan to Work Beyond Retirement," Dr. Phyllis Moen, 2001, Ithaca, NY

The Age Bubble is a critical human resource issue that employers must face because of the overwhelming number of baby boomers approaching retirement. Unless the boomers are retained in the workforce longer, there will be a shortfall in employee numbers due to a reduced number of workers coming through the ranks. 44 percent of the world's people live in countries with below replacement fertility levels. (Andrews, 2002).

## Need for New Strategies

In the next 40 years, the number of Australians aged over 65 will rise from 2.4 million to 6.2 million, with the proportion of older people doubling to 25 percent. Towards the middle of this century, after the baby boomers have retired, there might be only 2.5 people of working age for every person over 65, compared with more than five people currently.

"An Age-Old Problem," Karen Kissane, *Sydney Morning Herald*, April 20–21, 2002, p. 30

The growing ranks of older workers are not the only shift that will be taking place in the workforce. The proportion of younger workers is also shrinking. According to the Bureau of Labor Statistics, workers aged 25–44 will decline by 3 million, dropping from 51 percent of the labor force in 1998 to 44 percent in 2008, while, over the same period, workers aged 45+ will increase from 33 percent to 40 percent of the workforce, an additional 17 million workers (Dohm, 2000).

The most successful companies ten or even five years from now will be those that have adapted their policies and environments to meet the unique opportunities presented by their aging workforce.

Organizations today must implement strategies to address these future trends and capitalize on a multigenerational pool of workforce talent. How will your organization maintain a stable, motivated, and productive workforce as the needs of your employees continue to change and the pressure of the marketplace continues to reshape the way business is conducted?

Many leaders and HR professionals are so busy maintaining current business activities and preserving profits that they spend minimal time focusing on strategic planning for future employees.

No matter how large or small your organization may be, it is crucial to conduct the necessary research to identify how severely you will be affected by these demographic changes, to understand what needs to be done to survive and prosper in the new world.

---

We cheer roundly when older people demonstrate creativity, "can do" attitudes and athletic agility. An 88-year-old skier or tennis buff is looked upon with admiration and respect and may well be saluted in the media. Older celebrities are revered. But for the most part, esteem for seniors paradoxically ceases abruptly at the hiring gate.

What changes is not older peoples' capacity to be vigorous, productive, and creative. Rather, society is unwilling to see seniors as vital and active contributors far beyond traditional retirement age. It's assumed that people of a certain age suddenly turn senile and accept being seen as useless and dispatched to decades on the golf course, playing bingo or just plain idleness as a way of life.

It's obvious, of course, that no human of any age would choose to experience feelings of uselessness and devalued self-worth. Tales of men dying shortly after retirement are legion.

Why should we suppose that older people, whose way of life has been vital, interesting, and productive would not want to sustain that life as long as possible? Much of human dignity is experienced and expressed through work. As social creatures we need to feel valued and empowered, feelings which come from knowing we are contributing to our fellow humans.

In reality, we're facing a demographic time bomb. Yet we seem capable only of short-range vision. The scramble to boost today's productivity and this quarter's bottom line blot out concerns for societal and cultural shifts, which will affect tomorrow's productivity and bottom line.

Go60.com "Productive Aging in the 21st Century," Editorial by Robert Knechtel

Once upon a time it was the older workers who were more highly regarded in the workplace than the younger workers. However, over the past 15 years we've witnessed a turnaround whereby many older workers have been denied training and development opportunities and have been the first to go with downsizings, mergers, and other cost-cutting measures.

Some employers discriminate against older workers because of old-fashioned perceptions and myths relating to their abilities. With fewer people entering the workplace, organizations have no choice but to realize the importance of retaining these valuable workers to survive the changing work landscape.

According to the Equal Employment Opportunity Commission, which enforces federal workplace discrimination laws, the number of age-discrimination complaints filed in 2002 is nearly 25 percent higher than in 2000, making age discrimination the fastest growing EEOC category.

Staying Ahead of the Curve, The AARP Work and Career Study, A national study conducted for AARP by RoperASW, September 2002, p. 11

Sadly, the value of older people is widely underestimated, particularly when it comes to paid work. So many antiquated perceptions of older workers still exist within the workplace today, but the reality is older workers' positive attributes far outweigh the negatives. Most importantly, their experience can boost your organization's profitability.

In recent years, older workers have been leaving the workplace earlier, retiring as early as 50. Many people now need to work longer for a comfortable retirement. For many baby boomers, their retirement fund simply won't be enough. Obviously, if older workers remain longer in the workforce, this will alleviate much of the financial burden on other taxpayers.

## The Government Dilemma

Retaining mature-age workers is important to a country's economic future. A direct consequence of an aging population is the increasing old-age dependency on the economically active population.

---

Business, unions, and the Federal Government are joining forces to change the attitude towards older workers as companies fail to heed warnings of a labor shortage.

The Business Council of Australia has likened the massive cultural change required to the new mindset that evolved when women began entering the workforce en masse.

"We have got a very big shift to make to get employers to think about recruiting people who are 55-plus," the council's chief executive, Katie Lahey said.

"We have got to start educating people in the same way we did with women in the workforce. I don't think companies have given it a lot of thought yet."

"Looming Labor Crisis Puts the Focus on Gray Force," Sherrill Nixon, *Sydney Morning Herald*, October 2, 2002

---

Now that we can look forward to a longer life, the whole concept of retiring early cannot be sustained. Take, for example, the scenario of someone who leaves school at the age of 22 to enter into the workforce, works until retirement at the age of 55, and then dies at age 88. This means that the person spent 33 years in the workforce and 33 years in retirement. To ensure individuals facing this life pattern have a fulfilling, financially affordable and enjoyable retirement, substantial savings and a well-thought-out retirement strategy must be in place.

Sure, governments could entice people to have more children by offering a financial incentive for each child born. However, there will be a significant lag effect whereby workplace numbers won't increase immediately and we'll have to wait another 20 years or so before we see the effects of such an increase in population. We could revert to the work practices of the United Kingdom in the 19th century where children from the age of six were sent down the coal mines to work, but somehow I don't think that would be an acceptable work practice today!

Governments around the world are now faced with the future challenge of dealing with a much larger retired and aging population which, in effect, will mean that a smaller percentage of the population is working and paying taxes to fund the education and retirement of a greater percentage of the population.

A logical solution for world governments to balance their fiscal budgets is to increase taxes to fund this requirement. This, in turn, means that younger workers will have less of a chance to build up savings for their own retirement, which will surely reduce their motivation.

If governments, however, encourage individuals to remain working for an extra five years, these individuals will be paying taxes for an additional five years rather than receiving retirement benefits from the government. The net effect will be a significant contribution towards balancing the fiscal budgets of countries. Although this explanation simplifies the issue, it will obviously require careful planning to be certain that there are taxation incentives for older workers who wish to continue working and consideration given to how social security benefits are calculated.

Some countries are now making efforts to address the impact of the aging workforce. For example, Singapore is providing incentives to encourage organizations to hire older workers, such as wage support to encourage more suitable job opportunities for local workers over the age of 40 and assistance for those wishing to undertake career transition.

In Europe, Finland has led the way with its National Program for Aging Workers, which has improved employers' attitudes towards their aging workers, increased the retirement age and developed many positive improvements in the areas of part-time pensions and flexible work opportunities.

Following on from Finland's lead, Austria has introduced incentives to retain workers beyond statutory retirement age, and penalties for leaving the workforce before that age. In Spain there are now severe pension penalties imposed upon those who retire before the age of 65 and lifelong learning is encouraged through the introduction of a system of competence-based skill recognition, accreditation, and transferability.

In Australia in March 2004, I facilitated a round table discussion on behalf of the Ministry of Employment and Workforce Relations to address how employers could be encouraged to employ older workers and how to encourage older workers to want to work longer. Attendees included government personnel, major employer groups, and CEOs of public companies. The following recommendations were made:

- Educate employers to understand the changing demographics;

- Breakdown all perceived myths relating to older workers and challenge stereotypes;
- Allow access to retirement funds while still working;
- Encourage phased retirement and develop income tax adjustments to assist;
- Provide subsidies for organizations to provide training for older workers;
- Develop industry-specific strategies; and
- Promote "older worker" role models

The fact that this subject is now appearing on government agendas is encouraging and, hopefully, the aging population and its subsequent effect on the workforce will grow in importance. Governments must lead the way by introducing much needed changes as soon as possible.

---

*While 13 percent of American workers today are 55 and older, that figure will increase to 20 percent by 2015.*
Bureau of Labor Statistics, 2002

---

## The Changing Workplace

---

*The only thing we know about the future is that it will be different.*
Peter Drucker, Management Consultant & Author

---

It used to be that a corporation's objectives were paramount and employees had no choice but to fit in with these inflexible ideals if they wished to advance up the corporate ladder and remain employed.

From experience early in my own career with an Australian bank, I discovered that if I was to keep my job and be offered any sort of advancement within the bank, I was obliged to accept promotions and transfers each time they were offered, even if that meant working in different cities and countries around the world. Although it presented exciting and interesting career opportunities and life experiences, the bank gave little consideration to my own career aspirations (or the regular inconvenience of packing up and relocating my then very young family, usually with only a few weeks' notice).

Nowadays, employers are gradually realizing that employees are gaining more control over their careers and a different approach is required if good people are to be retained.

Baby boomers and mature workers have experienced many changes in the workplace throughout their careers. The concept of having a lunch hour, taking a coffee break and working nine to five all seem so anachronistic now. They're probably more likely to squeeze in a quick sandwich at their desk while working long hours, taking calls on their cell phone at all hours, as well as working most weekends.

These days baby boomers and mature workers seem to be working longer hours, have more responsibilities, and are not always provided with the necessary training or adequate pay. This is largely due to downsizing, rightsizing, rationalizing, and restructuring (or any other fancy name you care to use for organizational cost-cutting).

---

*In 1990 Americans worked an average of nearly one month more per year than in 1970.*
Juliet Schor, The Overworked American, 1992

---

The quote above is now over a decade old, so we can imagine just how much more we're working today than in 1970.

After witnessing many of their colleagues being retrenched with substantial farewell payments, enjoying themselves and, in some situations, even returning to the organization in the capacity of consultant or on a contractual basis and receiving better payment and conditions than before, it is no wonder those who remain feel rather envious. They feel more like victims than survivors!

Not only must we slow the desire of older members of the workforce to retire, but governments should ensure that financial incentives to retire early are minimized and incentives to continue working are maximized. At the same time, organizations must endeavor to attract, develop, and retain their younger workers, who will be increasingly in short supply.

The dramatic demographic changes that are occurring will have an impact on us all, both as individuals and employers, as we work through the next decade. Employment strategies must be rethought and, if we get it right, there will be positive outcomes for organizations and their employees.

As we become increasingly aware of the necessity to retain older workers, we must identify and understand the reasons older workers are motivated to continue working and to recognize and capitalize on their full potential. Old-age stereotypes and myths no longer apply, and we can't assume to know the desires and aspirations of older employees collectively. They must be respected and understood individually if we are to retain and motivate these valuable workers.

---

The mature and vintaged are all too often made to feel and appear as victims or deemed redundant, treated as inadequate or simply ignored. What happens to us when we reach 50 that makes us so apparently worthless? Why should anyone—any company, any recruitment agency, any industry have the right to tell us that because we've made it to 50, we can't think, can't work, can't remember, or don't have the knowledge, the ability to learn, the appetite to meet new and continual challenges?

Bernice Weston, Founder of Weight Watchers UK and Founder of AGEPOWER, UK

---

# 5

# What Boomers and Mature Workers Offer

## The Senior Solution

---

*I've learned that a winner is someone who sees a problem as a challenge and turns a negative into a positive.*
Shane Gould, Australian Triple Olympic Swimming Gold Medalist

---

In the near future, most companies will have more than 10 percent of their workforce population over 50 and will be looking to employ people over 65. With the enthusiasm of the baby boomers to continue being active and useful, employers must embrace this to maintain future success. With fewer people entering the workplace, older generations of workers need to be appreciated and respected so they willingly remain in the workplace.

As employers we need to understand and address the variety of needs and preferences of baby boomers and mature workers. In order to retain their services, we must:

- Introduce flexible employment arrangements;
- Provide training and development opportunities;
- Motivate staff with incentive schemes (not just monetary rewards);
- Address age bias in a constructive manner; and
- Promote intergenerational communication.

Mature workers can contribute to your organization through their experience in such areas as problem solving, decision making, tolerance for change, mentoring younger workers, as well as transferring knowledge to their future successors. They are often willing to do tasks with less broad appeal in exchange for flexibility in their job role.

The reality is the next ten years will be quite different than the last 30 years in motivating and retaining our workforces to maximize profitability. We must take the necessary steps now to achieve improved individual fulfillment and effectiveness, as well as improved corporate health. The decision to embrace and retain older workers will determine your corporate survival. Otherwise you may not have enough employees to support your organization.

## Work Motivators

After working hard all their lives, many boomers and mature workers who have adequate savings and fewer family responsibilities are now seeking to establish more of a balance in their lives through flexibility in their workplace.

---

In a poll conducted for AARP by Roper ASW, workers aged 45 and over revealed that both "soft benefits" such as adequate time off (86 percent) and flexible schedules (76 percent), as well as "hard benefits" such as health care benefits/insurance (84 percent) and good pension benefits (76 percent), as "absolutely essential" parts of their ideal jobs.

"Americans are living longer and healthier lives, and represent an increasingly dynamic force in the economy," said AARP President James Parkel today in announcing the results of the survey. "The potential role for the 50+ worker in the future is even more exciting."

The survey involved 1,500 employed workers aged 45 to 74. It shows that workers 45 and over both want and need to remain in the workforce into their retirement years, thus filling a potential future vacuum in the economy.

More than three quarters (76 percent) of the workers said the fact that they "enjoy the job" or "enjoy working" is a "major factor" in their decision to be working right now, the same percentage which said that "need" for money is a major factor.

The survey also showed that a large majority (69 percent) of those interviewed plan to work in some capacity in their retirement years. More than a third (34 percent) of the total sample said they would work part-time for interest or enjoyment, 19 percent said they would work part-time for needed income, 10 percent would go into business for themselves, and six percent would work "full-time doing something else." Less than a third (28 percent) of the whole sample said they would not work at all, the poll found.

Those interviewed seemed conflicted over how big a role money played in their decision to remain in the workforce. A majority (58 percent) said that "economic need" is the "one major factor" why they work, but, at the same time, an overwhelming number (84 percent) said that they would continue working if "they won the lottery and were financially set for the rest of their lives."

AARP Survey Outlines What 45+ Workers Seek From Employers, AARP News Release, September 23, 2002, Washington DC

Popular reasons for why older workers choose to remain actively involved in the workplace include the following:

1. **Self-Esteem**

   Confidence and feeling proud of oneself are vital ingredients towards a happy life, and many older workers wish to continue working:
   - to be recognized as a useful contributor;
   - to be rewarded for achievements;
   - to be respected by coworkers and managers;
   - to use skills and abilities;
   - to draw upon experience;
   - to act as role models and mentors;
   - to stay busy (so as to not get bored from inactivity);
   - to partake in meaningful work;
   - to make a positive difference to the world; and/or
   - to be viewed by others as having a meaningful existence.

2. **Money**

The average age children move out has risen from just under 21 years to 25 in the past two decades—at a cost of $40,000 to $50,000 to the parents' retirement kitty. It is estimated that every year the adult child remains in the family home it puts a $10,000 hold in retirement savings.

"What If the Kids Won't Leave Home?" Deirdre Macken, *The Australian Financial Review*, February 16–17, 2002, p. 28

Retirement savings and government pensions may not provide enough funds to continue a desired standard of living or to cover various ongoing expenses. Older workers may choose to continue working to earn money:
   - to ensure they can maintain their desired standard of living once they do retire;

- to pay for vacations;
- to pay for club memberships;
- to cover mortgage or rent payments;
- to maintain the family home;
- to pay health-care costs;
- to take care of the added financial burden of caring for children who remain at home (and perhaps grandchildren) as well as elderly relatives; and/or
- to undertake youth-enhancing procedures.

---

In 2000, Americans spent $7.5 billion on cosmetic surgery. Sales of antiaging creams tripled between 1994 and 1998 and are expected to do so again by 2003.

David Stafford, "Acting Your Age," *Business Life, British Airways Magazine*, May 2002

---

3. **Environment**

   Often the environment in which older workers are employed can determine whether or not they are motivated to continue working. Reasons to remain working within the right environment include:
   - to work in friendly surroundings;
   - to interact and have open communication with workers (of all ages);
   - to work within modern facilities with up-to-date technology;
   - to feel a sense of being an important part of a community; and/or
   - to remain working closely with long-standing friends.

4. **Training**

   The importance of providing training cannot be underestimated. Specialized training provided by an employer should make sure that individuals are prepared for changing conditions in the workplace. Motivational factors to partake in training include:
   - to be seen as a useful team member worthy of investment;
   - to be up-to-date with technology;
   - to learn something new and use their brain; and/or
   - to make a strong ongoing contribution to the success of the organization.

5. **Flexibility**

   By offering flexible working conditions, it enables workers to pursue their desired work/life balance. Reasons for wanting flexibility in the workplace include:

   - to take on reduced responsibilities by having slowdown strategies available;
   - to work reduced hours if desired;
   - to take time off when required;
   - to be provided with career and retirement planning;
   - to have time and energy to have fun outside of work;
   - to feel refreshed when coming to work; and/or
   - to phase into a planned active retirement while still working.

## Work/Life Balance

*Don't forget until too late that the business of living is life, not business.*
B.C. Forbes, Scottish Journalist

A favorite saying is "Life is not a dress rehearsal, it's the main event." We are currently on the stage of life, and we'd better enjoy it because there's no second act. All work and no play? Forget it!

With increased pressure in work environments across the world over the past decade, many people have unintentionally entered a role that comprises work only, and have not had time or energy for life. For many, their life has been unintentionally put on hold in the foolish belief that there will be plenty of time later to enjoy it.

There are too many tragic examples where people have worked hard all their lives, only to die or become ill when they finally decide to wind down and start to have a life. This is usually because they have forgotten how to enjoy life after an all-encompassing and draining work period.

Today, I believe, we all need to seek and achieve a satisfactory work/life balance, and we need to work on it with as much effort as we do our job.

The following points will assist you to understand what boomers and mature workers prefer to focus on away from work in order to appreciate the work/life balance they strive for:

1. **Good Health**
   - To remain physically and mentally healthy

- To interact with others
- To continue to learn new skills
- To stay active
- To reduce medical expenses
- To avoid incapacity
- To truly enjoy the many options available in life

---

Exercise may well hold the key to the fountain of youth. Besides boosting longevity, getting fit is one of the most important steps older adults can take to maintain their mobility, independence, and quality of life. Gone are the days when growing old gracefully meant slowing down and taking it easy. For the 77 million baby boomers born between 1946 and 1964, it means just the opposite. Inactivity, not aging is the culprit behind chronic conditions such as heart disease, obesity, and osteoporosis. The good news is there is a lot you can do to delay or prevent them.

By 2030 one out of every five adults will be over 65 as boomers enter their seventies and eighties. As baby boomers age they are rejecting the notion that aging is synonymous with being frail and inactive.

Alliance for Aging Research, Washington D.C.

---

2. **Time with Family**
    - To play with the grandchildren
    - To help the next generation progress through life
    - To provide support to needy relatives
    - To spend more time with their wife/husband/partner

3. **Leisure Activities**
    - To play sports
    - To travel
    - To enjoy hobbies
    - To undertake physical exercise

4. **Further Education**
    - To undertake studies of interest
    - To complete an online degree or diploma course
    - To learn new skills
    - To have relevant/up-to-date skills

5. **Not For Profit Work,** such as
    - Charity work
    - Church groups
    - Coaching a sporting team

- Environmental involvement
- Volunteering for a worthy cause

During my time with DBM, I have worked with many people going through career transition following the loss of their job. Often, this was the first time since leaving college that they actually had time to think about what they really wanted from life as a whole, not just their career.

In 2001, DBM conducted a study called "Career Choices and Challenges of Younger and Older Workers" where they surveyed people on Outplacement programs in the 51 countries in which DBM operate, and asked them if ideally they would like to work full-time or part-time. The result was striking:

- 31 percent of mature workers said they would opt for full-time work if they had a choice, with many of the remaining 69 percent preferring to work part-time if possible.

The clear message from this research is that the majority of experienced workers want to work, but they also desire a "work/life" balance. Most have been working hard (and paying taxes) all their lives and seek to balance their lives and find time for outside pursuits to achieve a healthy mix of work and leisure.

---

Self-stereotypes of aging, or older individual's beliefs about old people as a category, do not appear to fit into the stereotype-threat framework. The underlying reason is that self-stereotypes of aging seem to develop and operate through internalization. We believe older individuals' internalized age stereotypes contribute to the formation of their self-perceptions of aging, which, in turn, can have a physiological outcome.

The lengthening of the average American life span by 27 years over the last century has provoked considerable research on the determinants of longevity (eg. Perls & Silver, 1999; Rogers, Hummer, & Nam, 2000). Much of this research has focused on genes (eg. Pletcher, Houle, & Curtsinger, 1999; Rogina, Reenan, Nilsen, & Helfand, 2000). Yet as much as 75 percent of longevity may be due to nongenetic attributes, including psychological and behavioral factors (Vaupel et al., 1998). In addition, most of the research on predictors of survival has focused on negative factors (eg. disease, injury, and cognitive decline; Stroebe, 2000). Relatively few studies have examined positive factors, such as beneficial beliefs, that might affect survival.

The increased life span of 7.5 years in our study is considerable, especially when we compare our findings with those of other longevity studies. The effect of more positive self-perceptions of aging on survival is greater than the physiological measures of low systolic blood pressure and cholesterol, each of which is associated with a longer life span of four years or less (Friedman et al., 1995). The survival advantage of more positive self-perceptions of aging is also greater than the independent contribution of lower body mass index, no history of smoking, and a tendency to exercise; each of these factors has been found to contribute between one and three years of added life (Fraser & Shavlik, 2001).

Accordingly, our study carries two messages. The discouraging one is that negative self-perceptions can diminish life expectancy; the encouraging one is that positive self-perceptions can prolong life expectancy.

Unfortunately, a vast majority of employers are not considerate of their employees' desires. As the workforce becomes older and the need to retain the baby boomer and mature workers is paramount, we must seriously consider and address these valuable workers' needs and wants. By identifying and appreciating what the older generation can offer and contribute, the need to introduce more flexible employment arrangements becomes clear.

The Boomers are the world's movers and shakers, and the world's biggest consumers. Now they find themselves sandwiched between the responsibilities of supporting young children or multiple families, and caring for aging parents. The shine seems to have gone out of their market segment as marketers shift their attention to the more "glamorous" groups, such as the Net Generation. But the Boomers will be back, emerging in demographic terms alone as an important age group worldwide. The key point is that, unlike their parents, they will remain young at heart. They will turn the mature market into vibrant midlife, or even mid-youth. As their responsibilities to parents and children gradually diminish, they will spend on cars, sports, cosmeceuticals, well-designed clothes, youth-enhancing products, adventure holidays, entertainment, and more. Always remember: the Boomers want to have fun.

"Boom On," Mike Durham, *Viewpoint Magazine*, Netherlands

## Skills and Attributes

The good news is that the baby boomers and mature workers have plenty of skills and attributes. Business leaders have much to gain from making certain that they have a clear understanding of the following offerings:

1.  **A wider skill base**
    Gone are the days where a person has the same job for life. Chances are a worker aged 50+ will have experienced:
    *   Working in many different job roles (either within different organizations or within various departments of the one company); and
    *   A variety of work experiences under different economic scenarios.

    Therefore, a number of significant and varied skills in several areas of activity can be brought to bear in their current role.

    Experienced workers often get a sense of déjà vu when facing challenges in the workplace. They are able to apply knowledge learned from past experiences to the current challenge or task at hand.

2.  **Broader experience**
    As a result of having worked in a variety of industries, corporations, geographic locations, and economic cycles, many experienced workers have a desirable and wide-reaching base to give value added to your organization. They can usually cope with responsibilities that stretch wider than their job specification.

    Baby boomers and mature workers can contribute by way of mentoring and being available to provide guidance and pass on skills to younger workers.

3.  **Wisdom**
    The expression "old and wise" has plenty of truth to it. We all make mistakes, even if we don't wish to admit it. But what's important is that we learn from our mistakes, don't repeat them too often, and become wiser.

    One of the best-kept secrets of experienced people is that, as they mature, they gain wisdom from simply living longer and having made more mistakes than a younger person. The longer we live, the more mistakes we make, and the wiser we become!

*It is the province of knowledge to speak, and it is the privilege of wisdom to listen.*
Oliver Wendell Holmes, Author

4. **Good work ethic**
   Of course, many young people possess a great work ethic. However, the point must be made that when we apply ourselves to a series of tasks for many years, we develop the habit of committing to our work in a consistent and more methodical manner, which, in most cases, helps to make work more enjoyable. There's plenty of evidence to show that most older workers possess a good work ethic, which ultimately leads to overall improvement in productivity.

Research conducted by Libby Brooke, a senior research fellow at La Trobe University (Melbourne, Australia), shows that older workers save companies at least $1,956 compared with younger workers, based on recruitment, training, absenteeism, and workcover costs.

Older workers are more loyal, staying with an employer for 11.4 years on average, compared with 4.8 years for younger ones.

"Looming Labor Crisis Puts the Focus on Gray Force," Sherrill Nixon, *Syndey Morning Herald*, October 2, 2002

5. **Greater perspective**
   Having gained wide experience over a long period, many older workers can visualize their organization's needs and challenges in a "macro" sense, taking into account the effect their decisions will make on the overall result for their department or company. Within this context they are also able to focus on the impact of their contribution within their own specific "micro" environment, such as their office, department, branch, store, or factory. By possessing a broader knowledge of the organization's operations as a whole, it is easier to identify what specific actions are required.

6. **Ability to adapt to new technology**
   We are now seeing baby boomers and mature workers embrace technology enthusiastically, as they realize how important computer skills are to fulfill not only their job

roles, but to do such things as online banking, researching, booking vacations, online shopping, or reserving tickets to a show. The stereotype that older workers are averse to new technology may have been true when computers were first introduced, but not so today for the vast majority of experienced workers.

7.  **Greater financial confidence**
    After saving money throughout their career, many workers experience an improved financial position as they get older, building up funds for retirement and reducing ongoing debts and obligations. (Not all experienced workers are fortunate enough to be in this position, but as standards of living continue to improve, the trend is progressing.)

    If people have financial flexibility and security, they are generally going to speak their mind more confidently and be prepared to make the right decision for their company rather than timidly respond in a way they think their boss expects them to for fear of losing their job. An employee who is prepared to stand up for what they believe in and communicate in a constructive way, is a real asset for any team or company. Whereas, if someone is under personal financial strain, it can possibly impact his or her objectivity to make the right decision.

---

*I don't know the key to success, but the key to failure is trying to please everybody.*
Bill Cosby, Comedian & Actor

---

8.  **Flexibility**
    Because of wider knowledge and experience, older workers are not so easily upset if their job role doesn't follow the script perfectly. From their wealth of experience they can confidently adapt, improvise, and make spur-of-the-moment decisions to address challenges and can demonstrate much flexibility in addressing problems that are out of the ordinary without creating any undue stress for themselves and those around them.

    While striving to achieve a work/life balance, many older workers may be willing to work in an environment that provides less security and may be happy to work on a casual or part-time basis, consulting on a special project or on a short-term contract basis or even embark upon job sharing. They may also be willing to undertake a less senior role, working fewer hours with less stress, even if it means receiving less pay.

9. **Fewer sick days**
   Research conducted with companies that have a large percentage of older workers often reflects a lower incidence of sick days. Employers are well aware of the huge cost to organizations that comes from paying for sick leave, as well as the subsequent impact on productivity if team members are away.

---

Extensive research has found no relationship between age and job performance. Americans age 55 and above take fewer sick days, adapt to new technologies successfully, and are more loyal to their employer than thirtysomethings.

"Productive Aging in the 21st Century," Robert Knechtel, Go60.com.

---

10. **Reliability**
    Because of more experience in the workplace, older workers can demonstrate a strong record of reliability and dependability. Having a career that spans many years, an employer can see a pattern of stability and dependability that can always be easily verified by reference checks if necessary.

11. **Alignment with aging customer base**
    No matter what industry you are in, the demographic shift is impacting your customer base. Aligning staffing demographics with your customer base makes sound business sense.
    British Telecom has worked to achieve this alignment and now has 19 percent of their staff aged over 50 (compared with the U.K. population of 20 percent over 50). A commercial advantage of matching staff with customers has been the invention of the "Big Button Telephone," which has proved to be hugely successful with customers with arthritis, or poor eyesight. Older workers have been more sensitive to older customers' needs.

---

People are much healthier in their 50s, 60s and even 70s than ever before, and there are more nonstrenuous jobs from which to choose. In the Information Age, youthful strength is far less important than a worker's knowledge, dedication, and experience—qualities that strengthen with maturity. The Commonwealth Fund, a New York-based philanthropic group, recently sponsored research to determine whether worker performance declines with age. While productivity did fall off slightly when manual labor was involved, researchers found no correlation between age and work quality among supervisors and professionals.

From AGE POWER by Ken Dychtwald, copyright © 1999 by Ken Dychtwald, Ph.D. Used by permission of Jeremy P. Tarcher, an imprint of Penguin Group (USA) Inc.

While mature members of the workforce may have a lengthy past, they also have a positive future. Look forward, not back. The result of understanding what baby boomers and mature workers offer, as well as what they actually desire within the work environment, will provide organizations with the ability to maintain highly motivated, flexible employees who will ultimately maximize productivity, performance, and profitability.

Mature workers and, in particular baby boomers, are refusing to age gracefully. They seek to remain an integral part of their organization and want employers to acknowledge their contributions and reinterpret the meaning of older workers. Provided they focus on maintaining their physical health and fitness, have a positive "can do" attitude, and a willingness to work hard, organizations have much to gain from employing these very productive people.

As the fastest growing segment of the workforce today, baby boomers and mature workers must be seen and heard if we are to appreciate and maximize their full potential.

## Experience Counts

A good example of a company that has learned the value of employing older workers is the Vita Needle Company, based in Needham, Massachusetts. The sign on the factory door states "Help Wanted. Light machine operators. Part-time. Employees set own hours/days. Predominantly senior citizens. No retirement age."

Why does Vita Needle hire seniors? In the 1980s, the company was pressured to expand its line of medical products due to the spread of AIDS. Initially it began recruiting older workers because they were reliable and inexpensive. In addition, management appreciated that 65+ workers were very careful and tended to have half as many work-related accidents as younger workers. Management also came to regard them as harder working, more loyal, and less prone to personal problems than many younger workers. Vita Needle's annual sales have grown by 20 percent every year for the past five years. Average age of Vita Needle employees: 73.

Similarly Travelers Insurance has taken a leadership role in using older workers by creating a job bank of temporary employees from a pool of retirees. The higher productivity of these workers has saved Travelers $1.5 million a year. General Electric has discovered that it is more economical to retrain veteran engineers in emerging technologies than to hire new ones. The Boeing Corporation regularly brings back capable retirees to help with new aircraft production. Likewise, Bonne Bell, the cosmetics manufacturer in Westlake, Ohio, created a "Seniors Only" production group—the brainchild of chairman and CEO Jess A. Bell, himself 74.

From AGE POWER by Ken Dychtwald, copyright © 1999 by Ken Dychtwald, Ph.D. Used by permission of Jeremy P. Tarcher, an imprint of Penguin Group (USA) Inc.

Don't think that productivity suffers as your workers get older. In fact, in most cases I've come across, productivity actually increases due to the fact older workers develop greater skills and experience over time.

Many companies around the world are now switching on to the fact that older workers can actually boost an organization's productivity. They are discovering that older workers are more committed, loyal, responsible, reliable and are great at dealing with people.

Tesco (UK) changed its policies and reaped the benefits of employing older workers. Out of the 150,000 retail workers, 21,046 are over the age of 50 and more than 1,200 are 65 and older. A company spokesman had this to say, "Tesco likes to believe it operates on meritocracy in which anyone can hold a job as long as they have talent. Tesco does not discriminate against, or in favor of older employees, but it does believe their experience is a vital asset. They can be better at dealing with people, both customers and staff, are more committed and loyal and are more responsible and reliable than young staff."

Wal-Mart Stores Inc (USA) also employs older workers, ranging from department managers to customer service personnel. Janet Wehner, Assistant Manager, said of older workers, "They are some of our best people because they really want to be here. They understand work and everything isn't about money for them."

Jon Ashworth, "Never Too Old: The Gray Revolution in the Workplace," *News International*, Times Newspaper Ltd. January 11, 1999

In 2002, the Westpac Bank in Australia initiated a "gray recruitment" scheme where they committed to train up to 900 recruits over the age of 55 as financial advisers and planners to cater to their older customers (around half their customers are over 46). Also, of the 600 staff at a major car rental company in Toronto, over 200 are over 65. They find that their older workers take better care of their motor vehicle fleet than their younger employees do. I know I'd feel much more relaxed about a 65-year-old driving my car than a 20-year-old.

In today's workplace, baby boomers and mature workers can remain productive within your organization if they demonstrate flexibility as well as a positive attitude, an energetic approach, and a willingness to share their experiences, yet be open to new learning. They can offer the following:

- A wider skill base
- Broader experience
- Wisdom
- Good work ethic
- Fewer sick days
- Greater perspective
- Ability to adapt to new technology
- Flexibility
- Financial confidence
- Fewer commitments
- Reliability
- Dependability to get the job done

It's time to wake up to the fact that being old really depends on the individual. Our age represents the years we've been on the planet . . . not a "use-by-date"! Employers must appreciate the usefulness of experienced workers in today's workplace. How do you want to be valued when you're older? As someone who can still make a vital contribution?

If there are people in your organization who are 60 and considered useless and/or under performing in their job role, there's a good chance they were useless back when they were 30. Don't use age as an excuse.

# 6

# Generations X and Y

## Making Their Mark

More than half of Gen X employees (53 percent) and the overwhelming majority of Gen Y employees (82 percent) plan to change employers in the near future, compared to 30 percent of Baby Boomers and 17 percent Matures.

*The Randstad North American Employee Review, Roper Starch Worldwide Inc., 2000*

As our organizations adapt to the changing demographics of their workforce, the need to retain younger workers becomes more apparent. With fewer people joining the workforce today, our focus must be on attuning employment and workplace strategies in order to entice and retain younger workers as active, loyal, and motivated team members.

Generation X is considered to be the generation that is now dominating the future leadership of companies. Gen X, specifically those born between the mid-60s and 1980, must be acknowledged and understood carefully to embrace their full potential. Increasingly, Gen X-ers are making an impact on organizations and, in many cases, proving themselves to be excellent employees and managers. They just want to do it their way. Gen Y-ers, those born after 1980 will also be a force to be reckoned with throughout this next decade.

There's no doubt that Gen X and Gen Y are making their mark on the corporate world. These generations are adding a new dimension of thinking to the workplace and a measure of balance to organizations. However, Gen X and Gen Y aren't the first generations to make an impact on organizational makeups. As every generation comes of age and enters the workplace, it has a new, unique way of doing things. No two generations see entirely eye-to-eye. It was not so long ago that baby boomers were seen as aggressively and intentionally breaking all the rules. Every upcoming generation differs from previous generations, and older generations will always wonder why the younger generations want to break the rules and make new rules.

## Common Misconceptions

---

*A recent survey found that money was the fifth most common reason for job change among Generation X.*
Mercer Cullen Egan Dell, 1999

---

Not only are there many misconceptions in the workplace relating to the more mature worker, as we've covered, but there's also a lot of confusion relating to younger workers with common misunderstandings relating to these workers. For example, we often hear that younger workers:

- are unreliable;
- are easily distracted and have a short attention span;
- have a poor work ethic;
- prefer to live off their parents;
- don't work as hard as their parents' generation;
- have too many personal problems;
- don't want to work long hours;
- are money-motivated rather than career-motivated;
- have unrealistic expectations;
- don't respect older workers;
- are too individualistic;
- act impulsively;
- have less empathy with people experiencing problems;
- are unmotivated;
- possess little ambition; and/or
- don't listen.

Actually, some of the above points may apply to certain individuals in the younger worker bracket, however, they may also apply to some baby boomers and mature workers. The fact is that everyone should be considered on his or her individual merit rather than assume that members of a certain age group are the same.

From my widespread experience across many industries around the world, I am constantly impressed with the maturity, commitment, and work ethic of the young people I encounter.

## Work to Live Versus Live to Work

---

Bruce Tulgan, 39, author of *Managing Generation X: How to Bring Out the Best in Young Talent* and founder and president of the Rainmaker Thinking Inc. consultancy in New Haven, Conn., says that the Gen X style of blurring the boundaries between the workplace and the home, between the personal and the professional, fits well with the needs of the millennial corporation.

"In today's global economy, employees and their employers need to think about their working lives in a whole new way," Tulgan says. "Everything is turned on its head. Job security is not about stability; it's about mobility. The very same forces that are changing today's workplace are working on Gen X, and they are dovetailing."

Part of succeeding as an enterprise means successfully managing your staff, and these days that means working to turn your culture into a place the Gen X-ers will want to call home.

Robert Blackburn, 26, is a manager of application developers at Reynolds & Reynolds Co., an information management systems firm in Dayton, Ohio. Blackburn thinks the main difference between his generation and the company's older employees lies in the nature of their goals. "People my age tend to like change, to not want to be pigeonholed, to get a lot of different experiences, to be able to move across the organization," Blackburn says. "Sometimes older folks seem to fear change more. They want to master something and then stick with it exclusively.

Tulgan says that by listening more closely to Gen X-ers, companies can find the keys to success. "We are all moving into the workplace of the future together. It's all about competing for the best people. And the best people are thinking about their work lives in a whole new way. Employers have to lose their attachment to the old-fashioned career path. We can all learn from the emerging workforce and generation."

Managing Generation X, Mindy Blodgett, CNN.com, April 20, 1999

---

Most Gen X-ers and Gen Y-ers have grown up in a completely different world than their baby boomer or mature worker parents. Most have learned to adapt to change extremely well due to the ever-evolving circumstances they have experienced and witnessed throughout their lives, including the following:

- Parents/Grandparents losing their jobs
- Parents/Grandparents divorcing
- Employment relocation
- Corporate takeovers

- Corporate collapses
- Mothers reentering the workforce
- Technological advancements

Because of their exposure and adaptation to the changing world of work, these younger workers have much to offer organizations through their creative thinking, computer confidence, motivation to achieve career goals, and zest for life. They have more of a "rules were made to be questioned" rather than a "rules were made to be broken" attitude. To retain these energetic people within the workplace, we must fully respect and appreciate their motivation.

---

The children of the baby boomers—broadly, the under 30s—are creating a world view of their own, based on another radically different set of formative influences.

This is the generation who've always known that "girls can do anything" and that women can combine motherhood with paid employment. They've grown up with a high divorce rate. They are postponing marriage and parenthood: only five percent of today's young women are married by the time they are 20 (compared with 30 percent of boomer women). They have driven the birthrate to a record low.

In response to a tough and unpredictable job market, they've adopted a more flexible approach to work. They are more interested in a "lifestyle" than a treadmill. Rejecting the rampant individualism of the boomers, they have become intensely tribal creatures who use technology to maintain constant contact with each other.

Unlike the impatient boomers, the rising generation tend to postpone commitments—to a course of study, a job, a sexual partner, a political philosophy, a commercial brand, or a mortgage. This is the wait-and-see generation; their catch cry is "keep your options open." They see their parents' generation as too busy, too stressed, too competitive, too materialistic.

"Talkin' 'bout our Generation," Hugh Mackay, *Sydney Morning Herald*, January 19–20, 2002

---

As the traditional "job for life" models break down, it is no surprise that younger workers are skeptical when it comes to job security. They've watched their parents dedicate their lives to their employer, only to be retrenched with little recognition of their hard work or loyalty. Their parents' employers probably had little regard for personal responsibilities outside the workplace.

Because of this, the majority of younger workers strive for a work/life balance with a work to live approach, rather than a live to work approach.

Last year, when I was invited to speak to senior HR professionals in Korea on changing employment trends, the attitudes of their Gen X and Gen Y workers were clear. I assumed the main reason I had been asked to speak was to discuss solutions to assist experienced workers to get back into the workforce. However, I soon discovered I was there to assist younger workers understand and adapt to the changes taking place around them. Since the economic recession of 1997, there have been many variations in workplace practices. Many older workers have been unceremoniously let go after a lifetime of commitment to their employers. The majority of Gen X workers have grown up in families where their parents have experienced only one job in their working life and have witnessed, firsthand, the devastating effects on their families because of an unforeseen and unprepared-for job loss. They have become disillusioned and have lost all trust in corporations and certainly don't wish to experience career paths like their parents.

From similar circumstances occurring around the world, companies are now experiencing difficulties in retaining young workers (and potential leaders for the future). Gen X and Gen Y workers seek a better work/life balance than their parents and are no longer interested in the traditional career path model. Some employers are ignorantly still trying to entice them with the old concept of work in this new and uncertain time.

## Workplace and Career Preferences

Gen X-ers and Gen Y-ers want to maintain an element of control throughout their careers and will choose to remain with an employer if it fits in with their ultimate career path desires. Most younger workers are more than happy to put in the required effort to successfully achieve work tasks, but won't necessarily invest in working overtime just for the sake of it.

---

In today's vastly different workplace, the idea of what a "career" is has new meaning. For Gen X-ers, a career consists of an ongoing series of assignments or projects, sometimes within one company, but most likely with a variety of employers. While they consider themselves sincerely loyal to their employer, they nonetheless do not hesitate to change their situation to take advantage of new opportunities.

Historically, people left an employer to increase their pay and advance their careers. But now there's a third reason employees have for changing jobs: a concern they are falling behind the pace of rapid change.

The Randstad North American Employee Review, 2000

Whereas mature workers and baby boomers before them traditionally left career planning to their employer, Gen X and Gen Y workers are taking more control and have no misguided trust towards their employer. Younger workers entering a workplace today are likely to plan and control their own careers, want to know where the company is going, and generally are more entrepreneurial than boomers and mature workers were when they were of a similar age.

Workplace and career preferences of younger workers include the following:

- To use informal communication, such as an email or text messaging, rather than a formal letter or fax.
- To know the corporation's goals so that they can share in the overall vision of the organization.
- To work with the latest technology and be provided with regular training opportunities for skill development.
- Flexible work arrangements so that they can take time away from work if desired, for example, taking leave without pay, being able to work from home, or receiving time in lieu of pay.
- To work in a friendly environment, preferably with some work colleagues of a similar age with similar outside interests.
- Preferring not to be told what to do but rather have suggestions made to them.
- Wanting to be involved with risk taking and entrepreneurial activities where possible.
- To work in a comfortable environment, which often means the desire for a more casual dress code.
- To be able to express themselves creatively.
- To be financially rewarded for their efforts, either as an individual or as a team.
- Wanting to be listened to for their individual ideas, rather than being assessed as part of a group.
- To have the opportunity to learn from older employees.
- To make sure they have enough time to balance their lives with personal interests.

To succeed, younger workers know they must embrace change and keep up with technological advances. They want employers to demonstrate a respect for their desires by providing a flexible work structure with ongoing expansion and review of their role within the organization.

---

*There are two things people want more than sex and money. That is recognition and praise.*
Mary Kay Ash, Founder of Mary Kay Cosmetics

---

## Strategies to Retain Younger Workers

Being part of a flexible organization is important to retain Gen X-ers and Gen Y-ers. These younger workers seek employment in an environment that can easily adapt to the changing world of work, enabling them to be provided with the support and guidance to advance in their careers confidently and successfully.

Some useful tips to retain younger workers include the following:

1. **Don't overmanage.**
   Allow younger workers to come up with their own solutions. Thinking through a problem and developing a solution is an important learning exercise and the experience will stay with them much longer than if the answer is given to them upfront. Even if they make mistakes, the learning experience is much greater than being told what to do.

---

*Where all think alike, no one thinks very much.*
Walter Lippmann, Journalist & Author

---

2. **Suggest rather than tell.**
   Gentle supervision and guidance can be far more effective. Offering suggestions for improvement will bring about better results than just telling workers what to do.

3. **Make allowances for mistakes.**
   No one's perfect. We all make mistakes! A positive environment, where people are encouraged to openly share and

discuss learning experiences, can be a valuable training ground. An environment where mistakes result in humiliation and chastisement is the quickest way to destroy an individual's initiative and creativity, not to mention his or her confidence.

---

*When you judge another you do not define them, you define yourself.*
Wayne Dyer, Author

---

4. **Create the right environment.**
   Make certain that the workplace is professional, yet comfortable and modern and functions well. Assess whether the work environment can be better adapted or modified to suit those who work in it.

5. **Listen to ideas and concerns.**
   Often someone looking at a situation with fresh eyes and no preconceived solutions may result in a breakthrough to improved productivity.

---

*The real voyage of discovery consists not in seeking landscapes but in having new eyes.*
Marcel Proust, French Writer

---

6. **Reward and recognize achievements.**
   Workers of all ages want their efforts and achievements to be recognized and acknowledged. It's easy to say a few words of praise, yet there are many managers who don't seem to be able to bring themselves to do so.

7. **Offer a flexible work structure.**
   Allow time to be taken away from the office for personal development and interests. Carefully plan to avoid any possible disruptions to workflow.

8. **Encourage regular interaction with older workers.**
   Be sure that younger workers know who they can approach for assistance with problem resolution and that there are no preconceived misunderstandings relating to older work associates.

9. **Provide a mentor/coach.**
Create an environment where younger workers can work closely with and seek guidance from older members of the organization.

10. **Encourage open communication among workers of all ages.**
This has to be worked on and encouraged from the most senior levels of an organization to ensure that mutual respect prevails among all workers and that there is an environment with a strong intergenerational mix.

---

*It is better to debate an important matter without settling it than to settle it without debating it.*
Anonymous

---

11. **Keep promises.**
Managers must stay true to their word to establish trust.

12. **Communicate the organization's goals.**
The goals of the organization must be clearly articulated and available for all staff to review, understand, and share the vision. Younger workers are generally curious and wish to understand where the company is heading and want to be sure that the company's values align with their own.

13. **Provide access to relevant technology.**
Training requirements and equipment upgrades for these workers should be reviewed regularly.

14. **Recognize quality rather than quantity.**
The substance of a younger worker's work may be focused on actually solving a problem rather than overloading with irrelevant information.

15. **Provide challenging tasks.**
The greatest learning experiences come from on-the-job training, being given real tasks to complete, and solving problems necessary to improve profits.

---

*A buried talent is never a buried treasure. Talents become treasures only through use.*
Anonymous

---

## 16. Offer ongoing career development.

As most Gen X-ers and Gen Y-ers today are in control of their own career planning, they want to clearly understand available career opportunities.

When employees (of all ages) join British Telecom, a career/life plan is developed and then reviewed regularly, ensuring that employees make ongoing choices and adjustments to their role within BT, depending on their needs. This has proven to be an excellent retention strategy.

---

*Great people are those who make others feel that they too can become great.*
Mark Twain, Writer & Humorist

---

Thomson Learning's Sr. Vice President for Human Resources, Steve Mower, has found that younger people are attracted to companies within the Thomson Corporation that are perceived as "winning," "growing market share" and are "on the move." Thomson Learning has developed a number of successful programs that appeal to their younger workers, as mentioned in Chapter 2.

As baby boomers begin to retire from the workplace, Gen X-ers and Gen Y-ers are quickly making up the majority of the workforce. Innovative management techniques must be implemented to retain these valuable contributors to maximize your profitability. Professional and personal satisfaction for them means greater retention.

---

*I would advise young people of today to dream. I believe one must have a dream and it must be refreshed regularly or you lose it. It is that dream of youth that they shouldn't lose for it is only then that you know that it can be done. As we age we keep being told that it can't be done, and we listen and lose our dreams.*
Richard Imershein, Retired IBM Executive

---

# 7

# Embrace the Multigenerational Workforce

## The New Workplace

---

*We have come out of the time when obedience, the acceptance of discipline, intelligent courage and resolution were most important, into that more difficult time when it is a person's duty to understand the world rather than simply fight for it.*
Ernest Hemingway, Writer

---

As the labor pool grows older, multigenerational workforces in any one organization are likely to be the norm rather than the exception. We can no longer dismiss our mature workers as being of less use and only focus our attentions on the more energetic youth and future leaders within our organizations.

As companies persevere with their antiquated strategies that identify older workers to be the first to be shown the door whenever a downsizing is necessary (as well as the high-tech march continuing through our workplaces), young "up-and-comings" are making their presence felt in many management/executive committees as well as boardrooms. Their influence is having a marked effect on the way things are done, from working hours to dress codes.

These days it's not only the dot-coms who are embracing young managers. Management teams are being made up of increasingly diverse generations, and this scenario is getting more widespread every day. It seems more and more young managers are being placed in charge of multimillion dollar projects, departments, entire companies and, of course, older workers.

One of the clear impacts emerging from this "new broom" approach are the new management styles occurring, often without any clear-cut, well-planned transition strategy.

Although new methods of leadership are a natural evolution in the workplace, we must now prepare current management and future management to cope with future changes in the workplace. Business leaders must adapt to the different requirements for each style of employee and create an environment where tension and disagreement among the different generations is minimal.

---

*Whether it is research and development, company management, or any other aspect of business, the active force is "people." And people have their own will, their own mind, and their own way of thinking. If the employees themselves are not sufficiently motivated to challenge the goals of growth and technological development, there will simply be no growth, no gain in productivity, and no technological development.*
Kazuo Inamori, Founder & Former Chairman of Kyocera

---

When we reflect back on the past (or on what still applies in some countries), it seemed that people of all ages lived and worked in harmony. The young looked up to and respected their elders, and these elders had active roles within their communities. Each member of a community had an important responsibility working towards the success or survival of the group as a whole.

Sadly, over time, communication between the different generations seems to have deteriorated so that the diverse abilities, experiences, and needs of each group are no longer held in high regard. Once upon a time the children sat around the fire and eagerly listened to their grandparents telling tales of past experiences. These days grandparents and their grandchildren are more likely to communicate via a brief email, or text or voice-mail messages.

An organization's objectives used to be paramount, and employees had to fit in with these immovable corporate objectives if they wished to retain their jobs or advance up the corporate ladder. Little flexibility was offered, and if you didn't meet the requests and demands of your employer, your potential for promotion was severely hindered. There was every possibility you would remain stuck in the same job for the next decade, that is, if you weren't fired!

The new workforce is taking on significant change and, as we enter this new era, there is a need to break the old rules and set down more effective ways to work in the future so that all generations are understood, appreciated, and creatively and effectively combined within the workplace.

In recent times, so many changes have evolved within the workplace that there are no hard and fast rules regarding each generation. Each person is to be respected as an individual with his or her own particular style of talent and abilities. There's no such thing as a "one size fits all" approach.

---

*The art of progress is to preserve order amid change and to preserve change amid order.*
Alfred North Whitehead, British Mathematician & Philosopher

---

Now, in the same way employers choose to remove people from their organizations if they believe it necessary, so too are employees choosing to remove themselves from organizations if they believe it to be beneficial to their careers and work/life plans.

The way we work and plan our careers has changed substantially over the last 20 years. Leaders need to be acutely aware of the following dramatic paradigms:

| OLD WORKPLACE | NEW WORKPLACE |
|---|---|
| Have job | Do work |
| Office | Virtual space |
| Success = Career Ladder | Success = Values, goals, & competencies aligned (career lattice) |
| Authority | Influence |
| Status = Position | Status = Impact |
| Entitlement | Marketability |
| Loyalty to company | Commitment to work and self |
| Salaries & benefits | Contracts & fees |
| Job security | Personal freedom/control |
| Identity defined by job & organization | Identity defined by life circumstances & work performed |
| Bosses & Managers | Customers & Clients |
| Employees | Vendors, Intrapreneurs |

Many of these new values are self-evident, however, several deserve comment:

---

- Have Job $\longrightarrow$ Do Work
In the past we talked about "having a job." Today, even when a company formally employs us, we are far more likely to think of ourselves as independent vendors. We make choices about who we will work for and what working environments we will consider working in.

   "Having a job" is a passive pursuit. "Doing work" is an active process. The difference is fundamental and revealing.

- Office $\longrightarrow$ Virtual Space
Traditionally, we have gone to an office, a factory, or a shop to pursue work. Technology is changing all that. Cell phones, Internet access, intranets, and video conferencing now allow many of us to work from home, from the side of a swimming pool at a vacation getaway spot, from a client facility, from an airport lounge, from almost wherever we choose. The result is that we have much greater freedom to blend work life and personal life than was ever possible in the past.

- Success = Career Ladder $\longrightarrow$ Success = Career Lattice
Many baby boomers have felt pressure—from family, peers, or even from society in general—to secure a steady job, work hard at it, remain committed to the company and aspire to move as high up the corporate ladder as possible. In this life view, status has been seen as particularly important, and pride has been derived from achieving a senior level within a corporation. But the concept of aspiring to be a success within a company due to perceived external pressure is now dissolving.

   A newer definition of success revolves around our own ability to accomplish whatever we choose. In this view, we move on a "'career lattice" rather than a "career ladder." Moving on a career lattice gives us far more flexibility throughout our careers, allowing us to gain skills across a wide range of competencies rather than simply focusing on a career ladder bounded by one narrow stream of activity. Approaching work from the perspective of the career lattice opens doors to more sustainable employability by increasing our career options and improving our ability to consider and succeed at a wider range of jobs and responsibilities.

---

*We all have two choices. We can make a living or we can design a life.*
Jim Rohn, Author & Philosopher

---

Ultimately, in fact, the greater latitude embraced by the career lattice can help employees align personal values and goals with professional objectives, reinforcing and underscoring the value of achieving a balance between what is important at work and what is important in our personal lives.

- Authority ⟶ Influence
The old definition of work indicated that a job brought with it levels of authority which allowed one person to give instructions that other people were required to obey. In this view, a job title indicated a relative position of power and influence within an organization. Except in the most unusual circumstances, that authority was never to be questioned.

The new way of work is characterized by influencing through action. Here leadership becomes a function of skills, demonstrated achievements, clear competencies, and the ability to communicate the "why" of a decision or instruction. This ability to influence by our actions can lead to greater work satisfaction and greater achievements, both for ourselves and for the people who work with and for us.

---

*Hierarchy is an organization with its face toward the CEO and its ass toward the customer.*
Jack Welch, Former CEO & Chairman of General Electric

---

- Loyalty to company ⟶ Commitment to work and self
Loyalty has traditionally been an important corporate commodity. In the past, it was considered a two-way street. Employees were loyal to the company, and the company rewarded them with job security and, up to a point, steady career progression followed by a gentle slide into retirement.

That was a well-meaning and honorable intention on the part of companies around the world. But on one continent after another, there came a time when economic and competitive realities made it impossible for employers to continue to provide such security to their employees. These same employers began to understand that, in a newly competitive global workplace, their own continuing existence would be continually in question.

At first, and not at all surprisingly, many employees interpreted the shift to be a betrayal: "I worked hard for them all these years, and look what they've done to me." More recently, people have come to understand that we are not being deceived by our employers, but that this is simply the way of work in a changing world.

---

In fact, when we look at the differences underlying all these shifts from old to new paradigms, we find a single incessant theme: We are responsible for our own careers.

Workers of all ages are now more motivated to be sure that their skills and experience remain current and are becoming more entrepreneurial, taking command of their careers and their lives as a whole, giving less importance to loyalty, and looking out for what's best for them. This can more frequently mean transferring to another organization to fulfill career aspirations.

---

*Entrepreneurs see change as the norm and as healthy. Usually they do not bring about the change themselves. But—and this defines entrepreneur and entrepreneurship—the entrepreneur always searches for change, responds to it, and exploits it as opportunity.*
Peter Drucker, Management Consultant & Author

---

Witnessing world events or experiencing a personal crisis or tragedy can have an impact on an individual's attitude toward the future. It causes us to pause and reflect and question our life and, perhaps, jolt us into realizing there is more to life than just working.

Following the tragic events on September 11, 2001 many people have changed the way they live their lives because of the appreciation of how precious life is. I know of specific individuals who have decided to relocate, change careers, enjoy more leisure time, or pursue a more meaningful existence as a result of this event.

The reality is that most of us spend more of our awake time during Monday to Friday in our work environment than we do with our family and friends. Remember: Life is not a dress rehearsal. It's the main event!

---

*You cannot be really first-rate at your work if your work is all you are.*
Anna Quindlen, Journalist & Author

---

## Generational Differences

For a multigenerational workforce to succeed, we must fully understand what each generation desires within their place of work. In this way, we can consider the challenges and changes required to embrace the multigenerational workforce and provide the best environment for maximum productivity and profitability.

The differences in each generation may be subtle or dramatic. The fact is, however, we need to appreciate what these differences are to enable us to design flexible and effective work environments.

## DIFFERENCES BY AGE

(In descending order of importance. Italics indicate differences among all three groups.)

### WHAT THEY *SAY* IS IMPORTANT

| Under 30 | Age 31–50 | Age 51 and Older |
|---|---|---|
| Work/life balance | Work/life balance | Work/life balance |
| Financial rewards | Job security | Job security |
| Job security | Financial rewards | Financial rewards |
| Professional satisfaction | Influence/autonomy | Influence/autonomy |
| *Career advancement* | Professional satisfaction | Professional satisfaction |

### *ACTUAL* DRIVERS OF RETENTION

| Under 30 | Age 31–50 | Age 51 and Older |
|---|---|---|
| Career advancement | Career advancement | Pay-for-organizational performance |
| Pay-for-organizational performance | Pay-for-organizational performance | *Job security* |
| *Pay-for-individual performance* | Innovation and risk | Career advancement |
| Innovation and risk | *Professional satisfaction* | Innovation and risk |

### *ACTUAL* DRIVERS OF COMMITMENT

| Under 30 | Age 31–50 | Age 51 and Older |
|---|---|---|
| Pay-for-organizational performance | Pay-for-organizational performance | Pay-for-organizational performance |
| Strategic clarity | Strategic clarity | Innovation and risk |
| Adequate development opportunities | Influence/autonomy | Influence/autonomy |
| Innovation and risk | Professional satisfaction | Adequate development opportunities |
| Influence/autonomy | Opportunity for career self-management | Strategic clarity |
| Professional satisfaction | | Opportunity for career self-management |

"What Do Employees Really Want? The Perception vs. The Reality," developed by David Finegold and Susan Mohrman of the Center for Effective Organizations, University of Southern California's Marshall School of Business, in cooperation with Korn/Ferry International (January 2001)

A major difference that stands out between the generations is that the Gen X and Gen Y groups have a much greater focus on working to live, rather than living to work, although older generations are realizing the importance of achieving a work/life balance.

When workers reach their 40s, 50s and beyond, their aspirations in life can change because they've already had many accomplishments, achieved certain career goals, have greater savings, possess high self-esteem, and have fewer family responsibilities.

As mentioned previously in Chapter 5, baby boomers and mature workers today are increasingly deciding to pursue a more balanced life by continuing to work, although at a slower pace, or to work on a part-time basis, allowing them more time to pursue other interests. However, this may not be the case with all older workers, as some may still wish to work full-time and continue to advance up the corporate ladder.

From my experience working with people throughout the world on outplacement programs, it was evident that many of these experienced workers had a preference to work part-time rather than full-time. Unfortunately, the greater majority of employers are not offering this amount of flexibility within their work environments.

Older workers today are looking for ways in which to increase meaning and satisfaction in their roles, not just reap financial rewards. They may want to give back to the community, assist with the development of others, undertake study, or develop new interests and hobbies.

Often we hear of a young manager having difficulty managing older workers because of their reluctance to change and their refusal to take direction from someone who is younger and less experienced. Similarly, older managers may have difficulty in convincing younger workers that they are not set in their ways and they are, in fact, energetic and in touch enough to provide them with the best leadership.

The desires of workers of all ages must be recognized in order to effectively modify current employment strategies for optimum success. Nowadays, it is important for organizations to provide a suitable, flexible environment to enable all workers to remain highly motivated and therefore make a significant tangible contribution.

## Managing Older Workers

When faced with the responsibility of managing the older members of your workforce, it is useful to understand the numerous challenges that may be encountered.

1. **Communicate Performance Measurements.**
   Baby boomers and mature workers are discovering that tying themselves to their desks for 60 to 70 hours a week is having little impact on annual performance reviews. Chances are their boss hasn't been there to appreciate their efforts anyway. He or she is possibly working from home! For younger managers, the realization is on the flip side. If the issue of work-time flexibility is not addressed and understood, baby boomer and mature worker subordinates may assume their telecommuting young bosses aren't working at all.

   Baby boomers and mature workers have worked in an era where hard work and long service are rewarded with subsequent promotions up the career ladder. In comparison, younger managers are more focused on performance rather than hours worked or tenure. Younger managers will need to find a common ground and help mature workers to make the transition to the performance-based reward and recognition culture of today's workplaces.

2. **Nothing Beats Experience.**
   No matter what the qualifications of a mid-to-late 20s/early 30s manager, he or she cannot proclaim to have the hands-on experience of older employees. Young managers should recognize that this wisdom comes from the "school of hard knocks" and having made mistakes and learned from them over the years. By asking for advice or assistance from older colleagues, young workers are helping to rebuild older workers' self-esteem, and, at the same time, may see another way of addressing an issue that they hadn't thought of. A lot of value can be gained from older workers with years of experience, and a young manager can gain a lot of learning by recognizing this value.

3. **Speak the Lingo.**
   Gen X is the first generation to grow up in the technology era. Many were taught to use a computer at school, had computers at home, and have always known a workplace that uses computers. Often, there is a lack of patience between the younger generations and the older generations where

mature workers don't understand or have some resistance to new technologies. This is especially pronounced in communication styles. Older generations place importance on the formality of written communication, whereas younger generations are much more comfortable with an informal email. It may be necessary to compromise and perhaps develop a "business casual" communication style as an effective middle ground.

4. **Who's the Boss?**
   While older generations are accustomed to hierarchy and bureaucracy, younger managers tend to shun power structures and may hesitate in enforcing authority. Past mentalities have very much been "what the boss says goes," with a "top down" management style, whereas younger managers tend to be very flexible with their authority and expect that assignments will be completed without any pushing.

5. **Casual Attitude.**
   As Gen X managers increase their numbers in the workforce, casual attire becomes more commonplace. Casual dressing and a lack of formality can have a varied impact on different generations. For older generations, a casual look can be seen as an abolition of workplace professionalism and a temptation for productivity decline. For younger workers, however, formal business attire may be too stuffy and confining. They may feel more productive dressing in a way that they are most comfortable. This is a hard argument for a company to take on, given maximum productivity is key, providing they are not offending customers and are professionally representing the company. Again, flexibility and compromise is usually the key for Generation X managers, such as keeping casual work attire for one day, for example, casual Friday.

For managers in the position of managing older workers, recognizing and addressing the differences between generations will bring about an understanding that issues which arise can be resolved and that the impact on workplace productivity can be minimized as long as there is compromise. Diversity is critical for organizations competing in today's global marketplace.

## Managing Younger Workers

---

*Generation myopia is the mistake we make when we apply the values and attitudes of our own generation to someone of a different generation.*
Jane Jopling, "Understanding Generations," West Virginia University Extension Service

---

Many older workers wrongly view their younger work associates to be lazy with a poor work ethic when, in fact, they just have a different attitude towards work. In addition to the points listed in "Strategies to Retain Younger Workers," in Chapter 6, here are some suggestions for effectively managing Gen X and Gen Y workers.

1. **Communicate experience effectively.**
   We gain a range of life experiences as we mature, and at times it is possible to experience an event that is similar to something that may have happened in the past. Many older workers who possess a strong knowledge base squander it by the way they communicate to younger people. Having an attitude of "knowing it all" is the quickest way to turn off a younger worker.

   If, for example, you have ever uttered a phrase similar to any of the following, you have probably caused younger colleagues to roll their eyes:

   - "I've been a manager for many years, so I know!"
   - "Don't question what I say. I have far more experience than you!"
   - "When I was your age, I showed respect for my superiors and appreciated their knowledge!"

   Older workers should share positive work values without sounding like a know-it-all. Managers need to rehearse communication strategies because developing and practicing this skill allows business experience to shine through on its own.

2. **Don't micromanage.**
   Most younger workers are looking for challenging and interesting roles and enjoy being given short-term assignments where they can demonstrate their creativity. Managers usually get the best results from younger staff when they set parameters around the task, and then allow them the

freedom to complete the project in their own style, rather than micromanaging them. Good managers should look out for windows of opportunity to apply these principles.

3. **Provide career development.**
   As younger workers focus more on their own individual career goals rather than leaning on job security and their employers to provide opportunities, organizations should address ongoing career development to entice continued employment. When addressing training needs, managers should communicate with their young workers to discover their preferences.

---

*We must open the doors of opportunity. But we must also equip our people to walk through those doors.*
President Lyndon B. Johnson

---

4. **Offer flexibility.**
   Younger workers are often more productive if given the opportunity to work outside the traditional rules and regulations. In their pursuit of a work/life balance, many younger workers enjoy the opportunity to work from home and take leave to pursue personal goals. To effectively manage younger workers, it is advantageous to appreciate what inspires them to be at their most productive and provide flexible work arrangements for them to achieve this wherever possible.

---

*Ignore what a man desires and you ignore the true source of his power.*
Walter Lippmann, Journalist & Author

---

5. **Let them make mistakes.**
   By allowing more flexibility in the workplace, there are less limitations on younger workers, therefore providing them with more freedom to come up with creative solutions. If managers are to take a more trusting approach by stepping back and allowing younger workers to make many of their own decisions, the possibility of making mistakes increases. Managers need to be certain that they communicate goals and parameters clearly and then allow younger workers to come up with a solution. This may mean they make a few mistakes along the way. However, if managers monitor and

give feedback, there is every opportunity that they will assist their staff to learn and grow.

---

*Successful managers tend to be people who want to influence and control other people in order to get organizational work done, not in order to glorify themselves.*
Harold J. Leavitt, Professor of Organizational Behavior & Psychology

---

## Motivating the Multigenerational Workforce

---

*The world of motivation is changing. Traditional tools seldom motivate knowledge workers. They react stubbornly to force and control methods; appraisal and reward become less effective as the level of professionalism increases. The only thing that makes them run is the pleasure they have in their work.*
René Tissen, Professor of Business Management & Author

---

To realize the full potential of your workforce, an understanding of the generational mindsets is beneficial:

| | Working-Age Matures | Baby Boomers | Gen X-ers/ Gen Y-ers |
|---|---|---|---|
| **Employment Expectations** | Cradle-to-grave | On my terms | Entrepreneurial |
| **The "Office"** | Work at my desk | Work at home | Work "virtually" anywhere |
| **Relationship Between Work & Leisure** | Purpose of leisure is to recharge batteries for work. | Work now so you can play later. | Never the twain shall meet. |
| **The Home** | Multi generational | Nuclear family | Back in the nest with Mom and Dad |
| **Fun** | Saturday night "out" | Staying "in" | Surfing the Web "from anywhere" |
| **Financial Focus** | Save for a rainy day | Indulge | Invest in an IPO |
| **Icons** | Lee Iacocca | Ben & Jerry | Jeff Bezos |
| **Formative Years Identity** | Date and mate romantics | Flower children | Hip hoppers |
| **Millennial Mindset** | Batten down the hatches. | Live for today. | Prepare for the best. |

*The Randstad North American Employee Review* (More than 6,000 Americans and Canadians ages 18–65 participated in the study during November and December 1999.)

Gone forever are the days of a job for life. The concept of remaining in one job from the time a person leaves school right through until the day the person retires is virtually nonexistent, other than the rare exception of working within a family-owned business. Most organizations can no more guarantee their own existence within the next 12 months than guarantee job security for their employees.

For this reason, the concept of motivating a worker by offering job security and using the "carrot and stick" principle no longer apply. The old contract of work has gone, and the new contract is one of "interdependence," where employees are responsible for their own careers.

If orders are given from senior management without consulting with the people involved, the results are often disastrous. Often decisions are made in the boardroom without taking into account the impact of these decisions on the people affected. I'm appalled at the examples I hear in which the head office issues an edict of structural change within an organization via email. These people obviously have no concern or respect for their employees and deserve the resulting inevitable negative effects.

Employers now need to substitute job security with a new commitment to develop and train their employees. If employers need to lay off employees in the future, the employers have at least provided their employees with skills that will enable them to get jobs elsewhere. In exchange for this commitment, employees will usually work hard and commit to the company for as long as they are employed and understand the rules for a "contract of engagement," rather than a job for life. The best way to describe the new work contract is that the employer provides employees with ongoing training, flexibility and development to ensure sustainable employability.

---

The self-motivated employee used to wake up every morning eager to go to work—praying by working. Then, one day, he or she just decided to stay in bed. Today, people work to get rich, to have fun, to meet new people, see new places and be seen, to develop themselves or whatever. But, they no longer work out of moral obligation. Work is no longer automatically accepted as a good thing. Motivation is no longer taken for granted. We've moved from *have to* to *want to*.

*Funky Business*, Jonas Ridderstråle & Kjell Nordström, Bookhouse Publishing, 2000

---

An environment must be created so that workers of all ages can communicate their needs openly, be recognized for their achievements, have training and mentoring provided to them, and have the opportunity to work flexible hours, reflecting an understanding and respect for personal needs.

Individual definitions of what constitutes "career success" and "career satisfaction" change with age. We need to consider how these definitions impact current employment strategies.

A more flexible workforce means that employment commitments can be increased or decreased depending on demand, and reduce the likelihood of having to make large-scale redundancies during an economic downturn. The bottom-line impact of a flexible workforce can be significant over time.

Training programs are an effective way to provide information regarding the contributions and advantages each age group has to offer. Another way to overcome the intergenerational barriers is to conduct focus groups to air ideas and concerns as well as to assist workers to understand each person's value. Issues can be openly addressed and a clear work plan can be developed so that all generations can work in an enjoyable environment, which is ultimately beneficial to company performance.

We talk of self-management in groups, so it makes sense to create a guiding methodology to provide an environment to address all concerns so that problems are sorted out and not allowed to fester. Allow employees to voice opinions, feelings, and observations and provide them with the opportunity to contribute to problem solving within this environment. All workers, no matter what age, may leave an organization out of frustration if they are not given an outlet to express their views. They need to feel valued and given support for development within their work environment.

---

*The day people stop bringing you their problems is the day you have stopped leading them.*
Colin Powell, Secretary of State

---

If an older worker is encouraged to be involved in group discussions, it leads to an improved sense of worth and avoids conscious or subconscious disengagement, whereby a worker may give up and spend each day just going through the motions without making a significant contribution to company performance.

This type of giving up approach can be tantamount to sabotage in a company.

Often there is a lack of real commitment or focus from those who have their sights set on retirement, so we must involve them in a way in which they continue to feel as if their contribution is valued to avoid their productivity declining markedly.

In order to embrace the multigenerational workforce and engage employees of all ages in effective working relationships, we must make the necessary preparations to cope with these different groups to ensure mutual respect and appreciation.

---

Asked to list their key people issues, the CEOs of the Best Employees in Asia cited:

Developing and maintaining a high-performing, motivated workforce in the face of change.

Creating a performance-oriented culture while managing employee expectations; and

Effectively communicating—to reinforce the culture, to enhance employee motivation, to ensure employees know where the business is going, and to provide clear and direct accountability for employees.

Originally printed in Hewitt Associates Hewitt Quarterly Magazine, *www.hewittasia.com* or *www.hewitt.com*. Reproduced with permission of Hewitt Associates LLC.

---

## Bridging the Gap

We frequently have a tendency to assume other people think as we do and approach them as we would expect someone to approach us. This, of course, is not always the situation. One of the wonderful things about the world is that we are all unique human beings. In a management role, each generation responds in different ways, and all of us need to be very conscious of this in our dialogue with others.

---

*I've never seen a company that was able to satisfy its customers, which did not also satisfy its employees. Your employees will treat your customers no better than you treat your employees.*
Larry Bossidy, Chairman & CEO of Honeywell Int. Inc.

---

Workers of different ages value different aspects of their employment, however, most are motivated by the opportunity for self-expression, training opportunities, and career development. Organizations must not only offer flexibility and try to adapt to their employees' needs, but they must also respect their individuality. With the changing demographics impacting the mix of people who work in our organizations, it is necessary to understand how employees view their workplace to retain good people.

The impact within a company that does not provide the right environment for their employees will be that they will need to replace those who depart, including their potential future leaders, leading to much risk and additional cost.

An organization's growth doesn't just rely on capital expenditure, machinery, technology, the stock market, buildings, equipment, and motor vehicles. It relies on good people and having the right mix of people working together within productive teams. Employees of all ages must be encouraged to remain with your organization through the implementation of various incentives and initiatives.

The days of the inflexible employer are coming to an end. New strategies must evolve within the workplace to encompass this diverse, multigenerational work group. We need to bridge the gap between the old and the young, so that all may work effectively together. Employers today who focus all their energy on their younger employees without realizing the importance of their older workers will suffer in the long term. At the same time, it is important not to stifle the career aspirations of younger workers simply because older workers are staying around longer. We must appreciate the importance of getting the workplace mix right to be able to achieve effective progress.

---

Talent makes capital dance.

*Funky Business*, Jonas Ridderstråle & Kjell Nordström, Bookhouse Publishing, 2000

---

# Trust

## A Rude Awakening

---

*An army fearful of its officers is never as good as one that trusts and confides in its leaders.*
President Dwight D. Eisenhower

---

A few years ago I was contacted by the human resource manager of an international bank. She was seeking my assistance with a planned layoff for one of their senior executives, as part of a proposed restructure.

When I met with the HR manager and her CEO at their office, I could see that the CEO was decidedly nervous and felt rather uncomfortable about communicating the organization's intentions to the senior executive.

Apparently, due to a decision made by the head office in the United Kingdom to cut costs by restructuring that particular division of the bank, the executive was to be laid off, even though he had performed extremely well and was regarded as a highly productive employee. I asked whether there had been any mention within the bank of the proposed restructure, wondering if the senior executive had any idea of what was heading his way. I was informed that it was highly unlikely anyone would be aware of the situation, because of the confidential nature of the discussions that had taken place within the highest ranks.

I realized I needed to coach the CEO on how best to handle the meeting. I developed a script for him to work with to enable him to stay focused on the task at hand and make the announcement in the most effective and sensitive way.

Originally, he had planned to advise the executive that his services were no longer required on a Friday afternoon, which, I quickly informed him, was the worst possible time to do this. By laying someone off on a Friday, the person has the weekend to contemplate what has happened, usually without any support structure or ability to act, which can intensify negativity towards the organization and the person's own sense of loss.

The CEO reconsidered and chose the following Tuesday for the planned layoff to take place. The plan was for the CEO and HR manager to speak to the employee, sticking closely to the predetermined script. Then, immediately after being given the news, the then ex-employee would meet with me in the next office so I could provide assistance and support regarding his newly unforeseen situation and advise him regarding my involvement to provide outplacement services to support his career transition.

When Tuesday arrived, I provided further last-minute advice to the CEO, who appeared even more uncomfortable than in our previous meeting. I then waited while the meeting took place in the next room. After approximately 20 minutes, the HR manager opened the door and ushered in a very ashen-faced executive of about 50 named Ben.

I invited him to sit down, closed the door, and began talking with him. It was plainly obvious he was not hearing a word I was saying and was overcome with grief, quickly bursting into tears. Ben was experiencing many profound emotions all at once: anger, shock, feeling of failure, embarrassment, helplessness, uselessness, loss of confidence, loss of self-esteem. He was displaying the signs of a shattered man.

He couldn't understand why the bank had let him go without any warning, particularly after he'd been promoted consistently up the ranks throughout his 15 years of loyal service. Only two months before, he'd had an excellent performance review in which he'd received praise for his contribution to the bank and was awarded an attractive bonus and salary increase. His boss had even discussed with him a promotional opportunity in the near future.

It was clear that Ben was finding it difficult to take in the information I was endeavoring to communicate to him, so I provided him with thoughts and suggestions for getting through the next 24 hours, including how best to break the news to his wife, and to set a time to meet with him at my office the following morning. He assured me he was able to get home. I provided him with my home phone number in case he needed it and agreed that we'd meet again in the morning as planned.

At the conclusion of our meeting, I was horrified to discover there was someone waiting outside our meeting room to accompany Ben back to his office in order for him to clean out his desk immediately, hand over his keys, and escort him off the premises. Such a humiliating departure for a hardworking, dedicated employee!

In our meeting the following morning, Ben looked extremely tired and was constantly fighting back tears, shaking his head, not being able to understand how this could have happened to him. He told me how he had passed the news on to his disbelieving wife, and showed me his most recent performance review, which falsely gave him every reason to feel confident about career prospects and job security within the bank. For 15 years he had provided much loyalty and commitment, including working weekends, undertaking frequent business trips away from home, sometimes for long periods, as well as working very long hours.

Sadly, there was no discussion whatsoever between the bank's senior management to see if Ben's skills could be capitalized on and utilized elsewhere within the various divisions and locations of this international organization. Absolutely no consideration was given to retaining a good employee (that the bank had invested in significantly over the years). Costs needed to be reduced in the short-term, and the bank believed that laying Ben off was the most expedient way to do it.

Ben had trusted his employer and assumed they would be true to their word. Yet, because of a strategic decision and a need to increase profits in the short term, he was given a rude awakening by being dismissed.

Trust, built up over 15 years, was gone forever.

---

- Trust between you and those who work for you is a valuable coin—build it and spend it wisely.
- You build trust based on integrity—do the right thing, always!
- Once you lose the trust of others, you're going to have problems regardless of what other abilities you possess.
- Trust others as they trust you, but this doesn't relieve you of responsibility, so check on the things that count anyway.

William A. Cohen, Ph.D., *Wisdom of the Generals*, Prentice Hall Press, 2001

---

## Misplaced Trust

---

*Integrity without knowledge is weak and useless, and knowledge without integrity is dangerous and dreadful.*
Samuel Johnson, British Lexicographer

---

Regrettably, the above example of an employee giving many years of dedicated hard work to an organization, only to be unexpectedly notified that he is no longer required, is not an isolated example. Through various perceived cost-cutting measures, many organizations have mistakenly let good people go because of their affinity with short-term, instant fix, compulsions.

During my global involvement with the outplacement industry, I have witnessed innumerable examples in many countries of shock and surprise when hardworking, dedicated people are abruptly informed that their services are no longer required.

In many Asian economies, such as Korea and Japan, there had always been the noble belief that a job was for life. After leaving school, a person's career was often mapped out within the same organization until retirement. People's belief was that their loyalty to their employer would be recognized and repaid by their employer offering them continuous employment. Unfortunately, following the significant downturn in the Asian economies during 1997, all that changed.

Many Asian companies had every intention of continuing to support their employees through even the toughest economic cycles, as was their custom, and they believed it was the price they were prepared to pay for a stable and motivated workforce. However, following the economic downturn of 1997 and economies like Korea and Japan being opened up to the global economy by removing protection from competition, many organizations were given no choice but to reduce staff numbers in order to survive. The impact from this dramatic experience has made a marked and indelible change on the way of work in many countries in Asia today.

It seems few have escaped this wave of staff churn, from the most junior to the most senior, throughout the world. Trust has literally gone out the window. Although there have been few exceptions to this trend, virtually no sector of the global economy has been immune from this phenomenon.

Trust determines the quality of the relationship between people. And in a sense, trust is a chicken-and-egg problem. If you attempt to work on building trust at the exclusion of other chronic and acute problems, you will only exacerbate your situation. For example, one of the best ways to build trust is to work on the mission statement and to work on alignment issues. But if you try to do this while keeping a closed management style, your people will always be walking on eggs without much trust in your words.

Low trust spoils communication in spite of skill training. For example, in low-trust cultures managers usually come up with performance agreements, job descriptions, and mission statements that people don't buy into. And when they don't buy into them, they don't use them as a constitution; instead they try to set up policy and procedure manuals to preserve their jobs and build their pyramids.

The trust level—the sense that "I can trust you" or "You're a trustworthy person" or "You're a person who will admit to a mistake" or "You're approachable" or "You're open and teachable" or "If you make a promise, you keep it"—is a gut-level sense that really undergirds the rest. If you're fundamentally duplicitous, you can't solve the low-trust problem; you can't talk yourself out of problems you behave yourself into.

Trustworthiness is more than integrity, it also connotes competence. In other words, you may be an honest doctor, but before I trust you, I want to know that you're competent as well. We sometimes focus too much on integrity and not enough on personal competence and professional performance. Honest people who are incompetent in their area of professed expertise are not trustworthy.

Stephen R. Covey, *Principle-Centered Leadership*

The impact of such changes within an organization must be considered seriously. Trust that is misplaced is extremely difficult, if not impossible, to rebuild. Here are some real examples of how organizations have lost trust.

1. **Broken Promises**

   An organization undertook a restructure with significant resultant layoffs and advised the remaining employees that it was unavoidable and won't happen again. Within a year, a further round of staff reductions occurred, with the process being repeated again just over 12 months later.

2. **Corrupt Confidant**

   A long-term employee found that, due to personal and health reasons, he wanted to continue working for the organization but with reduced hours, possibly moving to a part-time role. He discussed his desire with his supervisor, who assured him his request would be considered. When the next round of layoffs occurred, he found himself on the list and lost his job.

---

*I cannot and will not cut my conscience to fit this year's fashions.*
Lillian Hellman, Dramatist

---

3. **Judgment Resentment**
   An employee disagreed with her manager regarding the decision to repair a product that had been returned by a customer, rather than replace it, and expressed her opinion that there was a need for improved customer service. This caused the manager to be displeased, resulting in the prompt departure of the employee.

4. **Insolent Ignorance**
   A career transition consultant in an outplacement company was instructed by her boss that she was to provide less face-to-face counseling to individuals she had been supporting as a cost-cutting measure to improve profit margins. Because of her heavily increased caseload, the consultant was obliged to follow the rules. An individual going through career transition who was extremely depressed and in desperate need to talk was unable to access the consultant and subsequently committed suicide.

5. **Indelicate Downsizing**
   An organization decided it had to downsize and lay off 20 people. With no indication they were about to lose their jobs, these 20 employees were herded into a room by the HR department, then advised via a videotaped recording from the CEO that their services were no longer required. This humiliating departure negatively impacted the performance and commitment of those remaining as management was no longer respected.

---

A friend rang last week to tell me that one of his business associates had taken his own life. A day or two later, he rang back to say he'd just heard of another executive suicide—the third in as many months from the senior ranks of a major financial institution busily downsizing itself.

The responsibility that goes with the act of retrenching people should weigh heavily on the conscience of any organization. People's mental health is often at stake, and the emotional trauma inflicted on them by being told they are unwanted can be incalculable, especially if they are receiving similar messages, simultaneously, from other directions (as they often are: once you're on the downhill slope, you can become pretty unattractive to those around you).

It's an almost impossibly tough challenge for an employer to find a way of reassuring a retrenched employee that he or she is still a valuable person, even if no longer needed in this particular context; an impartial counselor is almost mandatory. Indeed, any organization that doesn't offer professional counseling to the people it retrenches is guilty of gross negligence. It's too late to regret our insensitivity when someone we've "let go" decides to end it all.

"We didn't pick up the danger signs," people will sometimes say, defensively. Well, sorry, but dumping someone inevitably creates a health hazard for them, whether the signs are apparent or not. To assume otherwise is to ignore one of the most fundamental truths about humans: nothing else hurts us quite as deeply as rejection, and sometimes that hurt is terminal.

Hugh Mackay, Pick Up Versus Put Down, *Sydney Morning Herald*, August 31–September 1, 2002, p. 31

In the fight for improved profitability and corporate survival (and perhaps, to be frank, the survival of the CEO), trust has been the casualty of this war. Although job security seems to have dissolved, there is room to reincorporate some of the old work philosophies as well as introduce new strategies to strengthen and rebuild the trust of employees.

## The New Work Contract

As our world changes, our notion of trust changes with it—and not always for the better. Trust seems to be under attack today, not just in business but throughout society.

The "Me" mentality that characterized the yuppie phenomenon of the eighties was a recent example of this erosion of trust. The notion of a class of young people earning substantial (many would say excessive) incomes, and apparently having no goals beyond earning substantially more, became etched in the public consciousness. Here was a group that appeared to trust nothing beyond fancy cars and high living.

Characterizations like this are obviously the product of general-ization and stereotyping. But just as certainly, there was something going on here. The general scorn directed at the whole notion of yup-piedom suggests that society in general wants something more from its business community than just the bottom line.

I recall talking with a group of young investment bankers. I suspect each would have denied it, but I knew I'd entered a den of yuppies. I came away from the discussion with one overriding and unsettling memory.

To a man and woman, this group of bright, well-educated, energetic people insisted that the companies that employed them had no inter-est in them beyond their capacity to generate fees and commissions. Falter in that objective, they felt, and they would be dumped uncere-moniously. They were resources to be consumed.

There was no sense of trust in their work environment on the part of these young people, a situation caused, I think, by a lack of real trust on the part of their employers.

What kind of trust might both have pursued? Not the blind "We'll take care of you" variety, certainly. The October 1987 stock market crash (in whose wake the label "yuppie" became academic for so many people who lost jobs) showed just how impossible it is to support that definition of trust. You simply can't take a market trading 240 million shares a day, turn it overnight into a market trading 120 million shares, and tell people, "We'll take care of you." People are going to be hurt.

But I can't believe that the solution to this dilemma is to take the humanity out of the workplace and say in effect, "We don't—or we can't—care about you, we only care about what you produce. You're one more machine in this factory."

There is another way that accounts for both the needs of the marketplace and our needs as humans. It's a way that admits that life can be dangerous by saying, "If you don't produce, or if the rest of us don't produce, or if the stock market crashes, or perhaps even if someone crashes an oil tanker into an Alaskan reef, you may be out of a job."

But it's also a way that promotes a sense of community by announcing, "You're a part—an important part—of this organization. Ultimately, you're responsible to and for yourself, but you're part of this group, too. We'll train you, listen to you, value and reward your contributions, tell you how you're doing, and tell you how we're doing. We'll be open and aboveboard with you, and we expect the same in return."

William J. Morin, Trust Me, A Harvest/HBJ Book, Florida, pp. 101–103. Reproduced with permission by DBM Inc.

Given the changing nature of the workplace today, losing a job at some point in a career may well be more a rule than an exception. The notion of relying on an organization for job security has become obsolete, and we are now in charge of our own careers. Hard work, commitment, and loyalty no longer ensure employment longevity.

Organizations should encourage their employees to plan their own careers and take responsibility for them, therefore removing the reliance on the employer for their employees' security. As an employer, you may have every good intention when you say "Trust me, I'll look after your career" and really mean it, but the truth is that no organization can guarantee their own survival in this tough world of work we live in.

It is very difficult for many employers to accept and embrace the concept of helping employees plan and design their own careers. It seems to be removing control, and a possible outcome could be that employees conclude they will have a greater chance of career success elsewhere. Often employers resist investigating and addressing employees' career desires because they wrongly believe that if they are ignored they will go away.

However, by demonstrating your intention to assist with career planning and taking a more open, honest approach, it ultimately positions the organization as a preferred employer and enhances long-term retention strategies. Many workers may, conclude that remaining with the organization best fulfills their career aspirations.

---

*Those who preserve their integrity remain unshaken by the storms of daily life. They do not stir like leaves on a tree or follow the herd where it runs. In their mind remains the ideal attitude and conduct of living.*

*This is not something given to them by others. It is their roots. It is a strength that exists deep within them.*
Native American Writing

---

A healthy relationship must be developed between the employer and employee in order to develop mutual dependence and trust. In recent years, there has been an environment of mistrust in many organizations, where employers have held onto the concept of the old work contract, whereby the organization is only concerned with its own interests, therefore destroying trust via their quest for improved profitability. This anachronistic work contract is obsolete, and a revised work contract that is more relevant to our current world of work will provide more positive and enduring results.

The new work contract is one where the employer:

- believes in honest and open communication;
- provides training;
- develops appropriate skills and experiences;
- provides opportunities to expand knowledge;
- encourages employees to develop their career/life plan;
- demonstrates their intention and commitment to provide ongoing work for as long as a job remains integral to the organization;
- provides no guarantee about the length of employment; and
- doesn't make promises regarding future job security.

From the employee's perspective, according to the new work contract, a commitment of working hard for the success of the organization is undertaken.

Layoffs are often unavoidable for organizations experiencing tough economic conditions. For example, after losing one of their major customers, Cordukes Limited was forced to downsize one of its branch operations. Although they endeavored to reemploy staff within their other branches, many workers had to be let go. Management made it their priority to minimize the impact of this difficult situation and because those who were let go and those that remained clearly understood the reasons for the restructuring, morale and productivity was not damaged.

On a much larger downsizing scale, British Telecom has been forced to let go 160,000 people over the last decade. They've experienced no loss of work time through industrial disputes, as all people laid off were well looked after, communication had been strong, and all employees understood the difficult decisions that had to be made for the organization's ongoing survival.

If an employee needs to be let go in the future due to difficult trading conditions, the skills, experience, training, and career planning assistance provided will make sure they are readily adaptable and capable of obtaining suitable employment elsewhere in the marketplace. The employer has provided the foundation to ensure the individual can gain sustainable employment, and as a result, the employee remains motivated.

As a business leader in a role such as CEO, manager, or HR professional, it is imperative that you empathize with your employees and recognize what their job expectations are, as well as the possible consequences of an employee losing his or her job and the subsequent shock experienced by those who assumed "it won't happen to me." In order to rebuild trust within the workplace, an understanding of what motivates and demotivates employees is necessary. To assist with understanding the concerns of your employees, William J. Morin, in his book *Trust Me: How to Rebuild Trust in the Workplace* (A Harvest/HBJ Book), suggests the following questions for employees to ask themselves:

1. Am I making a real contribution?
2. Do I understand what's expected of me on the job?
3. Are my expectations in sync with those of the company, my boss, and my peers?
4. Do I know what the end result of my efforts should be?
5. Do I have a clear understanding of how these results are perceived and appraised by my boss?
6. Have I recently added anything to my general knowledge of the business or to the skills I have to offer?
7. Am I reaching out for new professional skills? Am I growing?
8. Am I careful about limiting the amount of time I spend on personal business during office hours?
9. Do I have a personal business plan for my career?
10. Am I thinking about the business?

You may wish to encourage your employees to address the above questions as a way of developing their career independence. Also, by giving respect and understanding to each employee's perspective within the workplace, it will provide a better understanding of what is necessary to maintain an enduring successful work environment.

Within the new work contract, organizations must address employee issues clearly and respond to them accordingly, to improve retention. Thomson Learning uses engagement surveys (climate surveys) to focus on the following three key areas:

1. To Stay—Why do staff want to stay?
2. To Say—They will say good things to others if they are happy!
3. To Serve—They will go the extra mile if they are engaged in their job and will provide superior customer service.

Each unit of Thomson Learning conducts these surveys annually, as they believe that if employees "stay," they will "say" and will "serve" and, as a result, will engage in the company and remain. The president of each business unit addresses the issues raised from the surveys and is required to demonstrate how improvements will be implemented to lift the performance of their unit (therefore building trust). Most importantly, Thomson Learning has found that the units with the highest survey score consistently achieve the highest profits.

This new work contract is a far cry from the "job for life" concept of the past, but is a vibrant, dynamic, and positive contract entered into by the employer and employee, where both parties are empowered to make decisions in an open environment of mutual trust. As the degree of trust improves, so too will corporate performance. Don't let trust become a forgotten word.

---

Trust within an organization is far more complicated and fragile than trust between, say, a consultant and a client. With a client, you can largely control the flow of communication. In an organization, people are bombarded with multiple, often contradictory messages every day. With a client, you can agree on desired outcomes upfront. In an organization, different groups have different and often conflicting goals. With a client, you know if there's a problem. In an organization, there's a good chance you don't, even if you're in charge. If things aren't working out with a client, either party can walk away. That's not usually an option for people in an organization, so they stick around. But if they think the organization acted in bad faith, they'll rarely forgive—and they'll never forget.

Trust within an organization is further complicated by the fact that people use the word "trust" to refer to three different kinds. The first is "strategic trust"—the trust employees have in the people running the show to make the right strategic decisions. Do top managers have the vision and competence to set the right course, allocate resources intelligently, fulfill the mission, and help the company succeed? The second is "personal trust"—the trust employees have in their own managers. Do the managers treat the employees fairly? Do they consider employees' needs when making decisions about the business and put the company's needs ahead of their own desires? The third is "organizational trust"—the trust people have not in any individual but in the company itself. Are processes well designed, consistent, and fair? Does the company make good on its promises? Clearly these three types of trust are distinct, but they're linked in important ways. Every time an individual manager violates the personal trust of her direct reports, for example, their organizational trust will be shaken.

As difficult as it is to build and maintain trust within organizations, it's critical. An established body of research demonstrates the link between trust and corporate performance. If people trust each other and their leaders, they'll be able to work through disagreements. They'll take smarter risks. They'll work harder, stay with the company longer, contribute better ideas, and dig deeper than anyone has a right to ask. If they don't trust the organization and its leaders, though, they'll disengage from their work and focus instead on rumors, politics, and updating their resumes. We know this because we have seen it happen many times and because a high percentage of consulting engagements that seem to be about strategic direction or productivity turn out to be about trust, or the lack thereof.

The building blocks of trust are unsurprising: They're old-fashioned managerial virtues like consistency, clear communication, and a willingness to tackle awkward questions. In our experience, building a trustworthy (and trusting) organization requires close attention to those virtues. But it also requires a defensive game: You need to protect trustworthiness from its enemies, both big and small, because trust takes years to build but can suffer serious damage in just a moment.

# 9

# Cultivating Culture with Effective Communication

## Getting the Culture Right

---

*Good leaders make people feel that they're at the very heart of things, not at the periphery. Everyone feels that he or she makes a difference to the success of the organization. When that happens people feel centered and that gives their work meaning.*
Warren G. Bennis, Writer & Educator

---

Effective CEOs, business leaders, and HR professionals take the time to understand the sociology of their workforce and believe in the importance of communicating effectively. However, getting the culture right and communicating clearly can often be challenging when wide-ranging age groups work together. Understanding and respecting each group for their differences and specific contributions goes a long way towards ensuring that nothing is lost in translation when communicating messages or values, and maximum desired effect is achieved.

One of the primary secrets of success within the workplace is having the right culture (or organizational climate). This invaluable asset makes certain that those employed by an organization share corporate values and are the right fit, therefore contributing strongly to a productive future. In order to appreciate and understand company culture and adopt effective communication styles accordingly, it is necessary to fully comprehend the intrinsic elements that exist within the workplace, including the following:

- Values
- Age mix of workers
- Workplace environment
- Management style
- Dress code

- Multicultural heritage of workers
- Technology and equipment
- Traditions
- Assumptions
- Decision-making processes
- Team environment
- Existing communication vehicles
- Environment of trust
- Performance management practices
- Motivators

Although an individual may possess suitable experience and relevant skills, unless he or she fits the culture of the organization well, the person's employment could be detrimental and disruptive. All employees must share the values of the organization to be sure of high commitment and productivity and must feel comfortable within their work environment in order to work to their full potential.

Effective communication is the conduit for shaping the organizational culture you desire. In order to be sure that messages delivered throughout an organization are understood clearly, it is necessary to appreciate the various communication styles that exist within the workplace.

---

To lead effectively, you must create a corporate culture in which people get used to communicating clearly and directly. Here's an innovative solution: Tell them *exactly* what you want.

Reprinted by permission of Harvard Business School Press. From *The Attention Economy* by Thomas H. Davenport & John C. Beck. Copyright © 2001 by the Harvard Business School Publishing Corporation; all rights reserved.

---

## Generational Values

---

*Be sincere and true to your word, serious and careful in your actions; and you will get along even among barbarians. But if you are not sincere and untrustworthy in your speech, frivolous and careless in your actions, how will you get along even with your own neighbor? When standing, see these principles in front of you; in your carriage see them on the yoke. Then you may be sure to get along.*
Confucius, Chinese Philosopher

---

With four distinct generations now working together within the workplace, we must understand the impact of combining different values and communication styles. Generational differences vary, and we can't assume that all Gen X-ers think the same or all baby boomers think the same. However, due to the many changes that have evolved over the past 70 years, there are obvious disparities between each generation, resulting in diversified communication styles within the workplace, which need to be understood.

Many business leaders are unaware of the multiplicity of communication styles within their workplace and therefore struggle to work constructively with workers within the various generational groups. Yet if understood and leveraged, these generational differences can be a source of creativity in the workplace and can provide a clearer grasp of how best to relate and communicate with each individual.

By understanding the values that motivate workers of different ages, we are better able to position ourselves to develop successful operational practices. To retain good people, it is critical to comprehend how their values align with organizational values and to recognize that each person's value system influences the way the person thinks and behaves.

In order to better understand the variety of values that exist within the workplace, the following offers a generalization relating to each generational group:

---

### Traditional generation (also known as Mature Workers)
This group values privacy, and sharing inner thoughts may be challenging. Members believe in hard work and "paying their dues" before their achievement is recognized. Their word is their bond and they value honesty. Communication, proprietary, and procedure are formal. This generation was raised in an orderly society having clearly defined roles and functions. Because they survived the Great Depression and WWII, this group is not wasteful and values saving and making do. They are hard working, economically aware, and generally trustful of the government. They are optimistic and willing to sacrifice. Patience is a virtue.

### Baby Boomers
This group grew up in a time of economic prosperity against a background of rebellion. They value peer competition and strive for challenge and change. Boomers, like Traditionalists, value hard work because they view it as necessary for moving to the next level. Traditionalists value it because it is the right thing to do. Boomers

enjoy climbing the ladder of success. This is a show-me generation, and body language is important. Boomers work well in teams and do not like having rules for the sake of rules. This group will fight for a cause they believe in. Health and personal growth are important. Boomers thought their parents' world needed an overhaul so they saw their role as one of questioning, justifying, and creating change. The workplace will be dominated by this generation until 2015.

## Generation X

This is the first of the "tech" generations. This group may be economically aware because members grew up with double-digit inflation and unemployment stress. Unlike their predecessors, they do not trust institutions for long-term security. This group can be discouraged about society, but they are adept, clever, and resourceful. They are comfortable with change and clear about the meaning of balance in their lives. They work to live, not live to work. They introduced diversity, thinking globally, and "fun" into the workplace. They work hard, and like Boomers, want to rise on the ladder of success, but they do it mostly to be in control of balancing their lives. This group wants plenty of information. They value loyalty in the workplace, but loyalty can also mean giving "two weeks' notice." They like to manage their own time and solve their own problems.

## Generation Y

Called "Generation Why," this group has a firm desire to know the reason behind what is happening and what they do. This is a generation of mass world and interpersonal communication. Members are rarely impressed by new technology. They are optimistic about the future and realistic about the present. They have a good work ethic and could be close to the "Traditional Generation" when it comes to work. However, the motive for working hard is different. For example, they like to know why they are doing something and do not like to take blind orders. They like to see how they made a difference in others' lives or in their own personal life. This group questions "starting at the bottom" and feels the best person for the job should be the one who does it best. Seniority has to be justified and people have to earn respect; it is not automatic.

"Straight-line thinking" is a challenge for them because they believe it's okay to skip certain steps to achieve what they want. Having patience is really a challenge; they want to see immediate results and action. This is the group that will be impatient with the speed of downloading a document that would have taken weeks to research 10 years ago. It is important to note that this group includes present-day teenagers and those in their early 20s. Therefore, what's happening to them right now are the things that will influence this generation's future behavior.

Jane Jopling, "Understanding Generations," West Virginia University Extension Service

It's simple! If a person's value system drives his or her behavior, and a subset of behavior is communication, then understanding the different values of each generation provides a greater insight into how best to communicate with employees from each generational group.

Be aware that there is often a tendency to project our own values onto others, and care should be taken to avoid this. A diverse range of values within the workplace will build strength in your organization. Identifying and leveraging what each employee values can benefit an entire team. For example, there are some employees who:

- Value independence (You can rely on them to work hard with minimal supervision.)
- Value detail (These are your record keepers and those who instill order into your team.)
- Value innovation (These are your visionaries and creators.)

## Intergenerational Communication

*Differences in how individuals perceive and evaluate the world around them leads to distinct differences in how they gather information, approach problems, and make decisions.*
Carl Jung, Swiss Psychiatrist

Each generation has a favorite style of communication and by taking the time to gain an insight into these preferences, better communication can be achieved with employees of all ages. The differences in communication styles among the generations can be as diverse as personality types, and can be determined not only by age but by values and culture as well.

The following provides a generalization of each generation's preferred communication style:

**Traditional generation (also known as Mature Workers)** likes formal communication and tradition. Clear, concise messages are good, but short, curt messages may seem rude to them. Mailed letters or face-to-face contacts work well. Phone calls are OK also. This group may even read a newspaper or newsletter article. Many have email and cell phones, especially those living in urban areas.

**Baby Boomers** like messages that explain clearly what is happening without sounding like someone is controlling them. They like to be invited to share rather than watch. They want their questions answered without too many conclusive, direct statements. They respect letters, but they get overwhelmed with mail so they probably prefer email. They like phones and answering machines.

**Generation X** likes their messages in short, understandable bites. They may not deal too well with letters because they are not a writing generation. Email is perfect and chances are they have it. They like places for feedback and want to feel a part of whatever they are asked to do. Informal communication style is preferred. They use cell phones and depend on answering machines and voice mail. They may not read mailed newsletters, but they may scan electronic ones.

**Generation Y** likes concise action words. Emphasize that whatever you ask them to do is fun and worth their time. Humor can be used with this group to get a message across, but this group's humor may not be understood by other generations. This group likes all senses to be stimulated with colors, movement, and music. They want to respond quickly so email is fine. Instant messages on computers are a communication choice of this group. Although they are the youngest group, many have cell phones. Regular telephones are fine, too. Many in this group have never used a postage stamp.

Jane Jopling, "Understanding Generations," West Virginia University Extension Service

To illustrate just how different communication styles can be within the workplace, consider the following scenario:

Michael, a Baby Boomer, is the manager of a global marketing team. He is Canadian.

James is a product manager. He is a mature worker and is American.

Lisa is an e-marketing manager. She is a Gen X-er and is English.

Jessica is a marketing assistant. She is a Gen Y-er and is Australian.

Michael sends an email to every team member asking them to "provide a summary of key accomplishments for last year, based on their areas of responsibility." Here's what the team come back with:

- James submits a 15-page typed report, with copious amounts of detail, using 10 words when just one will suffice. He doesn't clarify Michael's needs. He mails it to Michael, given they work out of different offices. Michael receives it late as he only opens his "snail mail" once a week.
- Lisa calls Michael to clarify his needs so that she can tailor the information for this purpose. She emails him a one-page executive summary, with attachments that expand on the highlights noted in the cover email, so that he has this for reference and background. She also works in a different location.
- Jessica sends several instant messages to Michael to clarify his expectations, even though they work in the same office. She doesn't keep a record of his feedback because she received it in instant messages, so she relies on her memory. Jessica sends ten bullet points in an email, with no further explanation. She offers to provide the same information in a PowerPoint slide if Michael prefers.

Michael's response:

- He has received three reports, in three different formats, with varying degrees of detail.
- James's report is going to take him a significant amount of time to digest, refine, simplify, and summarize. He also needs to retype it as James sent a hard copy and can't remember where he filed it on his computer.
- Lisa's report is the most comprehensive and appropriate for his needs. He appreciates that she called to clarify his expectations. He's pleased that his input and her probing enabled him to receive what he needed. He can easily adapt her content to complete his report as she provided a Word document attachment in an email.
- Jessica's report is too brief and missing some of the feedback he provided. He feels frustrated because he thought he had given her appropriate guidance. It also includes spelling mistakes since she had failed to use the US spell check (remember, she's Australian) in her haste to submit the report.

In conclusion, due to the various preferred styles of communication, Michael could have simplified this exercise if he'd considered the intergenerational mix of his team. By doing this, he could have provided a more specific email with clearer expectations, or followed up with each member, anticipating their generational communication differences.

---

As Jack Welch, former CEO of General Electric, stated: "Any company trying to compete must figure out a way to engage the mind of every employee." But how can a 20-something sales manager engage the members of his team who range in age from 23 to 68?

*Link & Learn* Newsletter, Linkage Inc., Burlington, MA

---

Tips for communicating effectively with each generation are as follows:

| | Gen Y | Gen X | Baby Boomer | Mature Worker |
|---|---|---|---|---|
| **Preferred Communication Medium** | • Use email, telephone or instant message | • Use email, telephone or instant message | • Use email, face-to-face, or telephone | • Use email, face-to-face, or telephone |
| **Message** | • Explain what's in it for them | • Give short sound bites or just the headlines | • Explain but don't direct | • Be clear and concise but not curt |
| **Sensitivities** | • Expressive and open with emotions | • Like to be involved in the process or decision | • Invite to share or express opinion | • Be patient and allow time for explanations and rationale |
| **Work Ethic** | • Good work ethic but need to know why they are doing something and how/who it will benefit; loyal to self | • Hardworking yet they work to live, not live to work; loyal to self | • Believe in hard work and strive for challenge and change; loyal to a cause | • Believe in hard work and "paying their dues"; loyal to the company |

## Message Management

---

Based on psychological type, two individuals may have similar or different decision-making styles and/or approaches to problem solving. When differences exist, they can be the cause of misunderstandings. This is because our own style of doing things comes to us so naturally that we mistakenly believe that others are like ourselves. That is, we believe that others see and approach things the way we do. When they do not (which is often the case), we are likely to find fault rather than examine our own biases.

Try to determine the primary style of the people with whom you communicate on a regular basis. As you do this, you will become more skilled in noticing how their styles differ from yours. You will also become more sensitive to the strengths and blind spots associated with your own style of communicating with others.

*E-Speak, Everything You Need to Know Before You Hit the Send Button*, Maureen Sullivan & Michael Bednarski, Ph.D., DBM Publishing, 2000

---

When employee satisfaction surveys are conducted, communication is usually identified as the number one opportunity for improvement. Messages must be communicated successfully to avoid confusion and mistakes that can be detrimental to productivity.

The single most important strategy to maximize the success of your business is to ensure regular communication with everyone who contributes to your organization, including the following:

- Employees
- Customers
- Vendors
- Media
- Stakeholders
- Analysts/Consultants
- The Board

To help you achieve this goal, the following should be considered:

1.  **Target your message.**
    Who is the recipient of your message, and what is important about it from his or her perspective? What's important to an institutional stakeholder may be different to what is important to your 50-year-old administrative assistant.

2. **Ensure Frequency.**

   Particularly during times of change, you need to over communicate important messages. It has been reported that
   messages need to be reinforced up to seven times before a
   recipient hears and understands what is being said. This is
   particularly true if you are restructuring or merging, as there
   may be a lot of anxiety in the organization.

3. **Be Consistent.**

   Consistency is key to getting your message across. Don't tell
   one part of the organization one thing, and another something else. Maintain consistency between internal and
   external communications, and align these messages to the
   organization's values and culture to make them mutually
   reinforcing.

4. **Choose to Listen.**

   Talk less and listen more. You might already be a good listener, but perhaps you are selective about what you hear and
   when you choose to hear it. Be conscious about how you are
   using your listening skills and listen even deeper to truly
   understand what employees are endeavoring to communicate.

---

*Men are born with two eyes, but with just a single tongue, in order that
they should see twice as much as they say.*
Charles Caleb Cotton, English Author & Clergyman

---

5. **Solicit feedback.**

   Implement checkpoints to test that key messages are being
   heard and understood. Conduct 360-degree employee satisfaction surveys by garnering feedback on the company's
   business strategy and value proposition from different audiences such as customers, employees, and stakeholders.

6. **Use multiple channels.**

   Whether you're communicating via email, in person, on the
   phone, or through your company's intranet, leverage different channels to communicate your message in new and fresh
   ways. Consider how you can support your key messages and
   values in your internal rewards and recognition programs.
   Remember, reinforcement is key to the success of the
   message getting through.

7. **Be visible and available.**
   Direct and regular access to you as a leader will enable employees of all levels the opportunity to check and validate information they have received.

8. **Lead by example.**
   Demonstrating your desire to communicate effectively by respecting the individual style and preference of those you are communicating with sets a good example for others. Communication styles are infectious.

---

*The real art of conversation is not only to say the right thing in the right place, but also to leave unsaid the wrong thing at the tempting moment.*
Lady Dorothy Nevill, Society Hostess, Horticulturist

---

## CEO Speak

---

*Communication skills and style influence perceptions of a leader's competence.*
Stanton Crenshaw Survey

---

CEOs have a major responsibility to be sure that they communicate effectively with everyone within their organization, including all employees and those who influence the business, such as customers, stakeholders, reporters, and analysts.

Some tips for CEOs to maximize their role as a leader through effective communication are as follows:

- Be face-to-face.
  Whenever possible, communication should be face-to-face or, at least, verbal (via telephone or teleconference). Directly delivering the message will increase the chance it will be received and understood. Personal delivery provides an opportunity to reinforce the message with nonverbal communication as well as to strengthen a relationship of trust.
- Be strategic and consistent.
  Reinforcement of key messages is essential, in multiple mediums, and to varying audiences.

- Seize the opportunity.
  Use opportunities such as good news, bad news, or a change event to strengthen communication. But don't overcommunicate with "mission critical" news that is not, as this will dilute the receptivity and perceived quality of messages.
- Use anecdotes.
  Use anecdotes (or "war stories") to illustrate and support points being made, leveraging firsthand experience to build credibility and trust.
- Temper your emotions.
  When times are bad or when experiencing tough times or frustrations, don't sit in your office and send out random and "off the cuff" emails. Be planned, strategic, and consistent, and always be sure to temper your emotions. CEOs need to be perceived as stable and reliable—not emotional hotheads!

---

- To win battles, succeed in fund-raising, build a business, or succeed at anything else, you must communicate.
- Issuing orders is the easy part—the hard part is to make certain they are implemented as you want.
- If your orders are not understood and are therefore performed with errors, you are like the cartoon character Pogo, who said, "We have met the enemy and they are us."
- Don't try and fool those who would follow you by telling them something which is untrue—they'll know, or find out.

William A. Cohen Ph.D., *Wisdom of the Generals*, Prentice Hall Press, 2001

---

**Improvement Solutions**

CEOs, business leaders, and HR professionals are responsible for ensuring effective, high-quality communication within their organizations. Communication must be regularly reviewed and evaluated in order to be sure that messages are not being lost in translation. Some solutions for improving communication within your organization include the following:

1. **Establish a review team for internal communications.**
   This team should be made up of people of all ages and work levels and have the responsibility of reviewing, critiquing, and refining messages being sent internally to employees.

Members of the team could be short-term and rotated so that many employees throughout the organization have an opportunity to participate over time. This is likely to increase their vested interest in company announcements.

2. **Develop a creative think tank.**
Again leveraging the talents of representatives from all generations and work levels, create a think tank that provides an open and safe forum to identify what communication styles are working, what's not, and what else can be implemented.

---

*The key to successful leadership today is influence, not authority.*
Kenneth Hartley Blanchard, Writer

---

3. **Foster mentoring relationships.**
Provide opportunities for employees of different age groups to partner together for mentoring and coaching relationships. They could be specific to an issue or a skill identified for development (technology skill transfers from a Gen X-er to a mature worker) or broader in nature (an informal sounding board). This will encourage a better individual understanding of generational communication styles.

Strategic communication that appreciates the individual style of the person you are directly communicating with can influence how your message will be interpreted, therefore maximizing the opportunity for a successful result. Employees who feel heard, understood, and valued and who have a clear understanding of the organization's values and objectives will work harder and produce more.

Potent communication provides the opportunity to develop and nurture the organizational culture you desire. By aligning your internal and external messages, and by creating a culture that reinforces your values and value proposition, you will be well geared to attract and retain the best talent in the marketplace, irrespective of your employees' ages.

---

*Communication is a skill that you can learn. It's like riding a bicycle or typing. If you're willing to work at it, you can rapidly improve the quality of every part of your life.*
Brian Tracy, Author & Consultant

---

# 10

# Developing Talent

## Identifying Your #1 Asset

Before WWI there was not even a word for people who made their living other than by manual work. The term "service worker" was coined around 1920, but it has turned out to be rather misleading. These days, fewer than half of all non-manual workers are actually service workers. The only fast-growing group in the workforce, in America and in every other developed country, are "knowledge workers"—people whose jobs require formal and advanced schooling. They now account for a full third of the American workforce, outnumbering factory workers by two to one. In another 20 years or so, they are likely to make up close to two-fifths of the workforce of all rich countries."

Peter Drucker, "The Next Society, The New Workforce," November 3, 2001, *The Economist.* © 2001. The Economist Newspaper Ltd. All rights reserved. Reprinted with permission. www.economist.com

The industrial revolution of the 19th century saw machinery substitute human labor in the pursuit of increased productivity. Back then, labor was in abundance and those operating machinery could be easily replaced. People became the victims of progress, and machinery was considered the major asset within organizations.

Now we work amidst advanced technology, automation, and artificial intelligence. Although these advancements have resulted in less manual effort, the difference between a good organization and a great organization is the quality of its employees. In many industries, traditional manual strength has been replaced by brain power, and the success of an organization is largely dependent on the specializations of the individuals they employ. It is the intellect, experience, specialist skills, and attitude of those who make up the human component, that makes people the organization's most valuable asset.

No doubt you've heard the following expressions many times during your working experience:

"People are our number one asset."
"The assets go down the elevator every evening."
"We aspire to have the best people."
"We are an employer of choice."

As much as these comments are extremely positive, they are frequently used insincerely by business leaders who pretend to support these statements for the sake of their shareholders, but don't actually do anything to subscribe to their words by taking an enlightened approach to people management and development.

So why is the most valuable asset so often overlooked when organizations consider future investment? Sadly, investing in the training and development of employees is not always high on the agenda. In the pursuit of reduced budget costs, the importance of sustaining a workforce capable of achieving targets now and in the future is relinquished for the sake of cost-cutting and short-term focus.

---

A workforce-management tool based on the premise that in order to develop and thrive, a corporation must identify its best and worst performers, then nurture the former and rehabilitate and/or discard the latter. It's an elixir that in these slow growth times has proved irresistible for scores of desperate corporate chieftains—but indigestible to a good many employees.

A. Meisler, "Dead Man's Curve," *Workforce Management*, July 2003

---

## Risk Versus Benefits of Ongoing Learning

---

*While we are postponing, life speeds by.*
Seneca, Roman Philosopher

---

In times of economic hardship, developing and training staff is often put on hold or even ignored completely. Even when an organization recovers from a profit downturn, it usually takes a year or two to recover lost confidence and consider progressive workforce development programs to be of importance and reinstalled. Then, if training is undertaken, the investment risk is considered high as it will take some time for the organization to benefit and receive payback for training. What if they invest in training individuals who decide to leave shortly afterwards, taking their newly obtained skills elsewhere?

So often training is overlooked within organizations when they are doing well. Many managers are afraid of "rocking the boat" and risking the stability of their current environment by further empowering their staff or changing their daily routine. Also, some find it hard to justify training expenditure because of the difficulty in measuring results and immediately gaining a return on investment.

A training and development embargo by senior executives is usually well intended for the sake of saving dollars, but by overlooking the importance of staff training and development, they are jeopardizing their organization's potency in the business world. If employees don't receive the necessary ongoing training required to be up-to-date with skills and industry trends in order to perform efficiently, the duration and intensity of a difficult trading environment will, no doubt, be extended. Lagging behind competitors becomes inevitable.

---

*You don't stumble into the future. You create your own future.*
Roger Smith, Businessman

---

What must be realized is that the tough times are when you really need your people to be properly trained and performing at their highest potential, due largely to the fact that profits are much harder to come by.

Sure, there is some risk involved when investing company money in training and development. However, if it is not considered a high priority and is overlooked, organizational profits are sure to remain lackluster.

Offering training to your employees will encourage them to remain with the company, because they are receiving personal development benefits as well as relevant skills to perform their daily duties confidently and effectively. Those organizations that do not provide learning opportunities for business and personal growth will inevitably be endlessly searching for replacement personnel at a huge cost.

Training and development must be a continuous and well-thought-out strategy to ensure organizations are well equipped to compete and succeed in our changing world of work. To ensure both short-term and long-term maximization of profits, it must not be a stop-start process.

---

*Education is the great engine of personal development. It is through education that the daughter of a peasant can become a doctor, that the son of a mineworker can become the head of the mine, that a child of farm workers can become the president of a great nation. It is what we make out of what we have, not what we are given, that separates one person from another.*
Nelson Mandela, Statesman and Former President of the Republic of South Africa

---

## Learning and Development

---

People are capable of continuous learning and development—if they are supported by policies and practices that encourage them to grow. Human beings are exquisitely responsive creatures who have thrived over time by adapting successfully and repeatedly to new challenges in the environment. Humans are capable of continuously building skills and capabilities throughout life—at a frenetic pace during childhood, and at a quieter but still impressive rate as adults. We call this position Capacity Building.

The important differentiator of success is not innate ability, but effective effort—which we define as effort based on tenacious engagement with a task, close attention to feedback about results, and continual adjustments in strategy based on that feedback.

The notion that differences in effort are the principal source of differences in performance has a strong basis in research. Extensive evidence supports the link between effective effort and the development of new brain capacity and high-levels of expertise. Neuroscience provides a simple model to help understand the mechanism: sustained effort builds mental capacity by changing the organization of the brain itself. The brain responds to engagement in new challenges by forming new mental circuits. In effect, it rewires itself, organizing already existing brain cells (or neurons) into neural networks. These networks, in turn, allow humans to organize complex, synchronized beh٤ patterns dedicated to particular tasks. The brain not only rewires e٤ ing neurons, but actually creates new neurons as well, which are tł added to the neural circuits. What is most astounding is that this process of "neurogenesis" is not restricted to early childhood, as previously thought; it occurs throughout adulthood as well.

Jeff Howard, Craig Sawin, Developing the New Manager's Mindset: Unleash Workforce Innovation and Maximize Productivity, Novations Group Inc., June 2004

Training is significant as it enables workers to obtain skills that not only maintain their employability, but allow them to compete effectively in the marketplace. As the demand for highly skilled workers increases, so too does the need for organizations to make sure their employees are equipped to take on responsibilities and ensure further corporate growth and success.

Learning and development programs for staff, no matter what their age or level is within the organization, need to be thought through and planned carefully. The best methods to boost skills must be identified, and effective training must be closely correlated with the desired outcomes for the organization.

It is estimated that annual money spent on training each worker in the United States aged over 50 is less than one-third of the amount spent on each worker under 50. This proves that organizations are overlooking the capabilities of these workers and that workers over 50 usually have many productive years ahead of them (perhaps another 3 years or 30 years). In a world where there's no guarantee that workers will remain with your organization for an extended period, no matter what their age is, why discriminate against those over 50 who have full potential to contribute? If three years' payback can be gained from an investment in training, it is surely worthwhile. Therefore, age should not be the prime ingredient when determining who should attend a training program.

*To maintain our dynamic economy and to fill the jobs of the 21st century, we must make the most of the creative potential and productive capacity of this growing segment of our society.*
President Bill Clinton, Proclamation Declaring National Older Workers Employment Week (1998)

Employers need to plan carefully how training dollars should be spent and who will gain the most from learning opportunities. Often, there is a tendency for CEOs, senior executives, or training staff to get enthusiastic over a specific group of training programs without any proper assessment of potential value and payback to the organization.

Specific programs need to be targeted for their relevance to the organization's needs. I have witnessed many examples in organizations where training programs were introduced, yet many of the attendees gained little or no benefit whatsoever, as their job roles did not involve the skills taught in the training program.

Many millions of dollars have been wasted by unnecessary training expenditure. So often people desire training because they want to impress the boss, or see it as a status symbol, however, the training programs they attend have little or no relevance to their job role. A CEO may attend a one week live-in training program at a prestigious island resort and think it is so great that she believes each of the ten people who report directly to her need to attend the same program also. If, however, a clear payback is not evident, don't do it. Training shouldn't be viewed as a job perk.

---

*Never mistake motion for action.*
Ernest Hemingway, Writer

---

There are very few generic-type training programs available that address and suit the needs of all workers. Programs must be identified or developed to meet the specific needs of individuals or teams to lift their competencies and allow them to accomplish their job roles in a more effective manner.

A rule of thumb often used in business to gauge the effectiveness of training is this:

- 10 percent of learning comes from reading books, manuals and other literature;
- 20 percent is derived from training programs for skill and product development; and
- 70 percent from on-the-job learning and being assigned to specific projects and real tasks to stretch and develop capabilities.

On-the-job learning must be the main focus for those organizations wishing to achieve ongoing success. By investing time and effort into developing people by assigning specific challenging tasks or projects, it pushes them forward, removing them from their comfort zone, and encouraging them to take risks. The sense of achievement from successfully accomplishing projects will provide workers with the confidence to take steps forward and move up the ranks to take on additional responsibilities.

On-the-job development requires a greater commitment from colleagues and supervisors, recognizing that during this learning process, senior staff need to take on coaching or mentoring roles to assist with projects. Although there may be short-term costs involved, this is a small price to pay for advancing so that both the organization and the individual benefit.

---

*What you do speaks so loud that I cannot hear what you say.*
Ralph Waldo Emerson, Essayist & Poet

---

No doubt mistakes will be made when learning on-the-job, however, if addressed immediately, these experiences can be the perfect opportunity to encourage open discussion and learn from the mistakes made. Learning from mistakes indelibly inscribes these experiences in our minds to avoid making the same mistakes again.

Unfortunately, in many organizations, the quick fix, safe route is to avoid taking risks, heavily criticize any mistakes that are made, and have the same people remain in charge of projects, rather than devoting extra time to develop younger employees under the watchful eyes of seasoned professionals.

Depending on job roles and development needs, each employee should have an agreed minimum number of training days per annum (a general rule of thumb is a minimum of ten days) and, whenever possible, be involved in the decision process regarding the practicality and applicability of the methodology to be used.

There is a vast range of learning opportunities available in the workplace today, such as:

* Informal, on-the-job learning from coworkers and supervisors
* Mentoring programs
* Training workshops with coworkers

- Business schools
- Attending seminars and lectures
- Coaching, to teach additional skills, share experiences, and be available for ongoing guidance
- Inviting professional experts to speak to motivate and inspire
- 24/7 online training
- Professional association training and qualifications

It is vital to look at the development needs of each staff member, no matter how junior or senior they may be, and customize training and development so that their specific job requirements can be effectively performed. A competency profile enables careful comparison of an individual's existing skills and competencies and addresses shortcomings and weaknesses related to their job responsibilities. It is beneficial to seek the employee's training preferences as well as seeking professional advice from learning organizations and industry associations. In fact, very few organizations develop in-house training sessions these days and usually send employees to outside learning companies.

---

*Ignore what a man desires and you ignore the true source of his power.*
Walter Lippmann, Journalist & Author

---

### Developing High Potentials

---

Although internal and external training were found to be the primary methods by which companies in Asia Pacific chose to develop leaders across the board, a somewhat different strategy was applied to developing high-potential leaders. In the case of high-potential leaders, developmental assignments are much more popular.

The top ten companies manage their best talent more actively and effectively, as compared to other companies. They identify high potentials more rigorously and selectively, better differentiate their compensation, provide the right kinds of developmental opportunities, and closely monitor their turnover.

Originally printed in Hewitt Associates Hewitt Quarterly Magazine, *www.hewittasia.com* or *www.hewitt.com*. Reproduced with permission of Hewitt Associates LLC.

If you have identified your high potentials, those who have demonstrated above-average performance and the right attitude to pilot your organization successfully, it is imperative to have the most appropriate programs in place to develop these people.

Future leaders must have the necessary industry and company knowledge to lead your organization. This knowledge can be gained through a variety of different forms of training, including in-house training programs, external training, coaching and mentoring. Regular communication, and honest feedback in the form of both formal and informal meetings is essential to develop a career path for these individuals.

Although good leaders come in all shapes and sizes, they do have one thing in common—trust! Building and maintaining trust is the key to effective leadership. But this must be nurtured and developed over time via open communication, good listening, active participation, and by demonstrating honesty and integrity.

Successful leaders for tomorrow's workplace will ideally possess the following qualities:

- Excellent communication skills pitched effectively at each recipient's level
- Creative and innovative
- Recognize what needs to be done and how to achieve it
- Passionate about the tasks at hand
- Strategic thinkers
- Always looking for new opportunities
- Familiar with all relevant aspects of the business
- Consistently dependable
- Work well under pressure and can cope with high levels of stress
- Moral
- Respect life outside of the workplace and encourage a balance
- Can motivate a team, leading by example
- Possess vision and competence to implement it
- Ability to allocate resources and implement strategies successfully
- Treat people fairly
- Can arbitrate successfully with disagreeing parties
- Minimize emotional reactions
- Look at the big picture, including both short-term and long-term results

After evaluating and identifying those with high potential for leadership and the specific roles they will undertake in the future, it's time to put a plan in place to develop and empower those individuals worthy of future promotion. If managed correctly, investment in these individuals will pay off. A serious commitment from the organization to provide them with the right training, guidance, and on-the-job experience goes a long way in demonstrating to key staff your allegiance and commitment to their success.

## Performance Management and Career Development Planning

Many HR measures look at the short-term indicators, such as program satisfaction, versus the long-term results. For instance, most leadership development programs fail to track the desired change in behavior in the first two years after a training session. The increased emphasis on measuring long-term change is one of the biggest improvements in leadership development in recent years, according to Marshall Goldsmith, best-selling author, executive coach, and co-director for the Alliance for Strategic Leadership.

"Companies have done a great job coming up with leadership competencies and profiles and communicating these values. Unfortunately, there's been the assumption that if they understand it, they will do it," Goldsmith explains. "Leaders need to be supported in their efforts to change with focused action plans and feedback that extends well beyond the initial leadership training."

Originally printed in Hewitt Associates Hewitt Quarterly Magazine, *www.hewittasia.com* or *www.hewitt.com*. Reproduced with permission of Hewitt Associates LLC.

Training is vital, but to ensure the desired outcome is achieved, it must be monitored and measured. The process of conducting a training analysis is extremely worthwhile, even if the result is inconclusive. It is often difficult to accurately measure the return, particularly if training is to assist with a change event, however, a performance management process can identify and measure the potential benefits.

Although there are many performance management models in existence from which to choose, it is important to adopt a model (or design your own) that fits your organizational requirements. When identifying which model is most suitable, be sure that the one you decide upon measures not only results achieved, but the development of competencies and skills needed to achieve ongoing results.

Performance management systems must be developed with clear goals in mind to assess how well a person has performed and for the employees and their supervisor to jointly plan what development needs are required. It is often beneficial to use a 360-degree process (obtaining feedback from not only immediate supervisors, but customers, coworkers and subordinates) to measure progress.

A good performance management model is one that is flexible and can be regularly modified to make allowances for career aspiration variances and desires of workers of all ages. One rigid system will not suit all employees, although many organizations today still apply the same performance review and career development processes to all their employees, regardless of their age.

Some employers choose to use performance management systems for remuneration purposes only (to justify a pay rise, pay decrease, or bonus payment). Others address both career development issues and remuneration in the same appraisal, however, it's worth keeping in mind that the impact of news regarding remuneration modifications may distract an individual from focusing clearly on necessary development plans.

Performance management systems must be treated as a priority for all employees from the CEO down, in order to effectively manage training and development requirements. The CEO should, in fact, be the driving force behind performance management appraisals, making sure that all staff recognize the relevance and importance of this process and that business goals are to be aligned and achieved.

Loyalty of employees should be encouraged and preserved as much as possible. All employees should know what opportunities are available to them within their organization. Creating a comprehensive career development plan together with employees ensures they fully understand future career advancement opportunities.

Unless performance management systems are designed specifically for each individual's unique situation, clear information necessary to measure performance and for future planning of strategic direction will be blurred. It is better to find out in advance if someone is planning to reduce his or her working hours to care for an elderly parent, is leaving to have a baby, or wanting to undertake full-time study. An open environment of trust must be cultivated when conducting performance management and career development planning so that employees can honestly share their career aspirations without being treated with disdain by their employer and to avoid any future unforeseen staff shortages. If respect for individual preferences is not communicated clearly, employees will continue to robotically fill out forms with the information they know their employer wants to hear, therefore eliminating any effectiveness of a performance evaluation.

Sadly, people often only confront their future aspirations when they lose their job unexpectedly. From my experience with individuals on outplacement programs, I often hear people wishing that they had the opportunity to go through the process of self-assessment while they were still employed so that they could be better prepared to adapt to change and successfully move forward.

The benefits of providing self-evaluation opportunities for employees include the following:

- Assist to clarify their employment situation in their own minds;
- Identify desired changes and aspirations;
- Motivate workers to continue working hard for the organization to achieve their goals;
- May result in workers feeling revitalized and embracing their job with renewed vigor, enthusiasm, and passion; and
- Greater productivity for the organization.

A person who is highly passionate and committed to his or her job will always generate much higher productivity than someone who is disillusioned and unhappy.

## Exit Interviews

---

*Many a man would rather you heard his story than granted his request.*
Philip Dormer Stanhope, English Writer & Statesman

---

When people do depart your organization voluntarily, it is important to obtain honest feedback in exit interviews. Not all organizations conduct exit interviews. Some organizations don't perceive these interviews to be of importance, therefore eliminating the fundamental opportunity to obtain an early warning signal and understand potential problems within their workplace. An exit interview is a window of opportunity to gain valuable feedback on why a person chooses to leave the employer and learn what the organization can do in the future to avoid a repeat departure. It is important to recognize what can be learned from employees who leave to reduce overall staff turnover, increase retention levels of remaining key people, and improve profits.

An exit interview conducted by a person's supervisor or manager is often of limited value. Often the boss will hear exactly what he or she wants to hear. A departing employee may see little benefit in being totally honest for the following reasons:

- The boss may be the cause for the person leaving.
- Most people don't like criticism.
- There's a good chance their next employer will conduct a reference check with this employer, so believe it is best not to 'make waves' and leave on the best terms possible.
- It is regarded as a useless exercise and why bother being honest when nothing will change anyway.
- May wish to disguise the true reason for leaving for fear of reprisal, such as harassment or being offered another job.

Outsourcing this responsibility is the most effective way to conduct exit interviews. That way an individual's anonymity can be respected, and they can open up and communicate their reasons for leaving without uncomfortable feelings of disloyalty, offending anyone, or fear of reprisal. It is an effective way for the organization to gain valuable feedback to learn and prosper.

---

"Organizations learn only through individuals who learn. Individual learning does not guarantee organizational learning. But without it, no organizational learning occurs."

Peter M. Senge, *The Fifth Discipline*, Currency Doubleday, New York, © 1990

---

# Future Leadership

## Leadership Predicament

The word *management* comes from Italian "maneggio/maneggiare" and the French word "manège," the training ring in which horses run around encouraged by a long whip held by the horse trainer. But what if the horses learned to run around by themselves? What if the horses actually do a better job at running around without the trainer, age 46.5, holding a whip and standing in the middle? Or, what if the horses have even figured out that in a surplus society with complete global competition there are probably more sensible things to do than to keep on running around in circles. If you try to break-in smart people, they will break-out.

People may no longer be so obedient, but that does not mean that leadership is redundant. On the contrary, the funky world requires limitless leadership. Take leadership away and you usually get repetition and reproduction. The organization becomes constipated, incapable of self-renewal.

A major role of leaders, anywhere and everywhere, is to infuse chaos into order. Meaningful leadership is about stirring the pot rather than putting on the lid. It is the job of great leaders to support the organization in combining order and chaos.

*Funky Business*, Jonas Ridderstråle & Kjell Nordström, Bookhouse Publishing, 2000

In recent years, our perception of leadership has deviated from its traditional meaning. The old definition of work indicated that a job brought with it levels of authority that allowed one person to give instructions other people were required to obey. In this view, a job title indicated a relative position of power and influence within an organization. Authority was respected rather than questioned.

Expectations on leaders to perform are now greater than ever. The traditional hierarchical structure in today's workplace is dissolving. There is no longer a place for a dictatorial boss.

Existing and future leaders must now be accessible and active team members who are prepared to listen and respond to ongoing change.

The new way of work brings with it the demand for a revised style of leader who can influence rather than order. Now we are moving into an environment where leadership is more of a function of skills, clear vision, demonstrated achievements, clear competencies, and the ability to communicate the reason behind a decision or an instruction. This ability to influence by actions can lead to greater commitment levels and work satisfaction for all members of the workforce.

---

The boss is dead. No longer can we believe in a leader who claims to know more about everything and who is always right. Management by numbers is history. Management by fear won't work.

*Funky Business*, Jonas Ridderstråle & Kjell Nordström, Bookhouse Publishing, 2000

---

Yet, not all leaders are prepared to embrace this new way of work, and insist on clinging to the world of yesteryear. Denial of a world that is changing and hanging on to old leadership methods is no longer viable as world economies improve and workers have more choices than ever before.

With approximately 60 million baby boomers potentially leaving the workforce throughout the next 15 years and fewer younger people joining to replace them, there will be a significant void in available leadership talent. As we embrace the rapid changes taking place in our workforce, necessary preparation to ensure ongoing leadership, success, and profitability are vital.

We have traditionally looked at our workers aged 25–44 as our future leaders. However, in Australia, for example, the available supply of employees aged 25–44 is expected to decline by 15 percent over the next 15 years.

In Singapore, the impact is even more dramatic. In addition to declining birthrates, many young, well-educated workers with accumulated savings are exiting the island country for greener pastures. In the decade between 1991 and 2001, the age group 15–24 declined from 20 percent to 13 percent of the total population, a dramatic shift in a very short period of time.

Those with potential leadership qualities must be identified early, developed, and retained to fill the shoes of departing leaders and be capable of taking the organization forward into new territory in an ever-evolving market place.

## Identifying Talent

A leader is defined as an employee who is influential in guiding and influencing the activities of others, as they relate to organizational and individual goals.

Originally printed in Hewitt Associates Hewitt Quarterly Magazine, *www.hewittasia.com* or *www.hewitt.com*. Reproduced with permission of Hewitt Associates LLC.

To state the obvious, unless the right people are in place to drive an organization, future success will be unattainable. So often this fact is not addressed pertinently and consideration of future leadership is deferred due to other immediate operational needs that are more pressing.

In order to identify what is required for future leadership, the following should be considered:

- What future strategies have been developed and need to be implemented?
- What is your growth plan over the next five years?
- Who are your competitors and what are they doing?
- What are the competency needs of the organization?
- The economic cycle, outlook, and environment?
- Job skill requirements?
- Cultural aspects and sensitivities?
- Current market trends and innovations?
- Succession plans?
- Corporate aspirations?
- Who are the retiring employees who will need to be replaced over the next five years?

Take a look at your existing staff. Is there a gap between the talent you need for the future and the talent currently available? Can existing staff members be trained to take on greater responsibilities, or do you need to also recruit from outside to be sure that you have fresh ideas and the skills needed to survive and prosper?

Are you aware of the experience, qualifications, personal interests, and aspirations of current staff members? In order to draw upon existing resources within the workplace, it pays to get to know your team, not just superficially from their résumé, but by probing and taking a firsthand interest and observing their talents. High-potential individuals may not be obvious at first if you don't do the necessary research. Seek feedback from your existing management team regarding who they believe has talent worth retaining and nurturing into a future leadership role.

Often someone is identified as not having the necessary abilities for future promotion within their current department, yet may ultimately prove more successful in an alternative environment. We must be open-minded and think creatively to recognize opportunities for people to excel, otherwise good talent (and potential profits) may walk out the door. How would you feel if you discovered a former employee succeeding within the ranks of one of your competitors, after departing your organization because he or she felt disgruntled about being overlooked for a specific role and the employee's skills and abilities were not fully appreciated?

---

The ability to process new experiences, to find their meaning and to integrate them into one's life, is the signature skill of leaders and, indeed, of anyone who finds ways to live fully and well.

Reprinted by permission of Harvard Business School Press. From *Geeks & Geezers: How Era, Values and Defining Moments Shape Leaders* by Warren Bennis & Robert Thomas. Copyright © 2002 by the Harvard Business School Publishing Corporation; all rights reserved.

---

In order to identify future leaders and implement a winning succession plan, those with high potential must be identified. Some traits to look for in trying to find high potentials in a large organization include the following. Do they:

- Respect organizational objectives?
- Perform successfully on a consistent basis?
- Fit and embrace the culture?
- Communicate effectively and constructively?
- Feel strongly motivated and demonstrate a willingness to go the extra mile?
- Respond positively to guidance?
- Cope effectively with change rather than resist it?
- Work well with fellow workers, and are good team players?
- Understand and respect company policies and procedures?
- Feel confident to challenge what is unclear (or what they disagree with) in a constructive manner?
- Enjoy learning new skills and seek opportunities to do so?
- Respect fellow workers of different ages and seek to learn from them?

- Desire success for the organization as a whole and understand corporate goals?
- Have strong skills, competencies, and core values?
- Get results consistently?

Another way to identify high-potential individuals and determine whether they have what it takes for future leadership roles is to assign them to specific projects or tasks where they are seriously challenged and have the opportunity to excel.

Tomorrow's leaders must be able to deal with change, predict future movements in the market, and cope with and motivate a multigenerational team. So, what people will your organization need to achieve the specific tasks required to increase future profitability and ensure ongoing survival and success?

## Succession Planning

---

94 percent of human resource professionals feel their organizations have not adequately prepared younger generations to step into senior leadership positions.

DBM Survey, North America, June 2003

---

No longer can we be complacent with regard to existing leadership. Those leaders, like all employees, may choose to leave an organization at any time because of enticement elsewhere, or as a result of planning and managing their own careers and deciding on a different direction (perhaps to phase down to a less stressful environment) or even retirement. Also, as much as we don't like to think about it, there's always the possibility of an unforeseen illness or death of an employee.

Do you have a clear plan mapped out so that every key employee (at least the top ten percent of your company) has at least two potential successors available if the employee leaves? Also, in turn, who will fill their shoes? A succession plan, carefully prepared and regularly updated, allows you to have a readily available replacement in the event of an unforeseen departure, therefore minimizing disruption and additional costs. The probability of a replacement being successful is often much higher if an internal appointment has been made.

In many cases, younger workers will ultimately have the opportunity of advancing into a leadership role when older workers retire from the workplace. However, Gen X and Gen Y workers aren't going to patiently wait until someone retires, and may choose to leave if the right opportunities don't open up for them to advance. Doing nothing and waiting for natural evolution is not the solution and will condemn the organization to a life of mediocrity where seniority is perceived as the only way to advance.

---

Management Recruiters Australia (MRA) says burnout among Gen X-ers is a serious issue—in the past six months about a third of thirtysomethings on its books have expressed an intention to make a radical career change or at least wind back the stress dial.

MRA's general manager, Margaret Locke, argues the sentiment shift among Gen X professionals poses significant challenges for employers. She says they are the key "revenue generating staff" and future business leaders.

"Staff hit their prime in their 30s when they are skilled, experienced and can really contribute to a company's bottom line," she says. "This is when management earmarks individuals to become future leaders and executives. Ironically, it is at this point that employers lose their talented staff, often through lack of planning."

Paul McIntyre, "Burnout Sends Generation to Exits," *Sydney Morning Herald,* January 10–11, 2004

---

By engaging in an open discussion regarding the development of an active succession plan, some older leaders may welcome the opportunity to phase down to a reduced level of responsibility, paving the way for more rapid promotion of younger potentials. This strategy ensures retention and minimizes the stifling of younger workers' aspirations.

Most importantly, the succession planning process must be driven by the CEO to be successful, and the CEO needs to be a very active participant in the development process.

Designing a dynamic succession plan allows younger employees to work closely with those they may someday replace, ensuring the transference of knowledge. Obviously, experienced managers don't want their younger counterparts breathing down their necks anxiously awaiting their departure for the sake of their own advancement. And besides, in this world of changing demographics, they may wish to continue to work longer, either at the same pace or with reduced responsibilities and hours, or to postpone retirement indefinitely.

By empowering potential younger replacements, providing them with training and development, and creating new opportunities for promotion, their desire to learn and be involved and valued will be fulfilled, which, in turn, will result in added loyalty and retention.

## Replacement Costs

Wise businesses replace capital equipment after a certain period of time. They calculate the cost of maintaining the machinery, anticipating the cost of replacing the units with similar or better machines at some period in the future. Are you calculating the costs of replacing your human capital? The risk with human capital is that the replacement period is more difficult to predict. However, good maintenance helps extend the life of both types of capital. Human capital maintenance includes a wide range of systems, services and initiatives that make you more attractive to current and prospective employees. Reducing employee turnover by creating a more attractive work environment can drive hundreds of thousands of dollars to your bottom line.

Employer of Choice ® Transformation Prospectus, The Herman Group, Greensboro, North Carolina, *www.hermangroup.com*

It can be a costly exercise if training and development are invested in an individual, only to find they go elsewhere or leave due to dissatisfaction with their job. In addition, when a good person leaves, it may also affect the following:

- Staff morale
- Future leadership planning
- Customer relations
- Career decisions of other employees
- Sales strategies
- Recruitment costs
- Specific ongoing projects
- The knowledge base of the organization
- Profits

In my past experience in the banking industry, I often found myself pondering over a balance sheet detailing assets ranging from property and equipment to computers and receivables. I soon realized that the actual value of these hard assets is greatly multiplied by the results of what people are capable of doing with those assets when motivated to achieve maximum results for the company.

The costs involved with replacing a valued employee should not be dismissed. To replace someone who leaves unexpectedly, on average, can be equivalent to six to nine months' salary, due to recruitment costs and induction and training of the new recruit to ensure that he or she can perform competently. Not only can an unforeseen departure interrupt workflow and create a gap in the company structure, but there is always a risk that the time and effort taken to find the right person could backfire if the new replacement proves to be the wrong person for the job. Often, this is not known for sure until approximately six months have passed.

We are now in an environment where most people can present very impressive and comprehensive résumés, through skills they have learned attending outplacement programs or enlisting the assistance of a friend. References supplied are always going to provide a positive endorsement of their skills. It is highly unlikely anyone would furnish a reference who would not praise the characteristics of the individual. The content of a résumé prepared by an individual is not always an accurate assessment of a candidate's attributes, which means it is very difficult to achieve a perfect score when selecting outside applicants.

The cost of losing good talent is much greater when we realize the "opportunity cost" of a person with much promise who may have contributed greatly to the organization for years ahead, possibly advancing to a senior leadership role. Often the issue of losing good staff is swept under the carpet, and management does not learn from the experience and address how best to retain their personnel.

Many times an excellent employee may choose to leave an organization due to limited prospects, yet once they have left, the remaining colleagues and managers demean and criticize the person as not being good at his or her job. What a shame "opportunity cost" cannot be reported as a cost item in the accounts so that a person's true value can be acknowledged and management can be held accountable for the cost to the organization when good talent is lost.

---

Well-known Omaha Steaks, based in Omaha, Nebraska, recently reported an additional $348,000 of profit to invest in opportunity areas. Where did it come from? According to JoAnn Kozeny, vice president of human resources, she was able to save that much money in recruiting, training and similar costs because employee turnover was under control at a lower level. The funds had been budgeted for her use, but were not needed. Healthy approaches to the maintenance of human capital can generate net dollars for the employer.

Employer of Choice ® Transformation Prospectus, The Herman Group, Greensboro, North Carolina, *www.hermangroup.com*

## Leadership Roles for Older Workers

*No man was ever so completely skilled in the conduct of life, as not to receive new information from age and experience."*
Terence, Roman Dramatist

Perhaps some of your older workers have been overlooked as leaders because of the common misconceptions about age and rigid retirement policies that are in place. What if these older workers would prefer to remain with your organization rather than pursue retirement? Their experience and understanding of your company's goals and objectives would surely be an asset in a leadership role.

If you examine the available talent within the mature end of your workforce, you'll probably realize some of these individuals have great problem solving skills and have the valuable resource of knowledge and experience to transfer to younger workers. Encouraging highly skilled and experienced older workers to embrace additional roles, such as that of mentor or coach, will allow them to take on strong leadership responsibilities, which will enhance their sense of worth within the organization, therefore resulting in increased motivation and retention.

Quite often, dedicated, hardworking people who have worked for the same organization for 20 years, find themselves made redundant because they don't possess the "necessary skills" for the challenges of tomorrow. Many organizations absentmindedly ignore the potential of older workers and deny them the opportunity of keeping skills updated. Technology is constantly evolving, and workers of all ages must be provided with the appropriate training.

One way to achieve cross-fertilization of skills and knowledge is pairing younger and older workers. If older workers are assigned as mentors or coaches to younger workers, their sense of importance and worth within the organization will be expanded and they will therefore be more willing to continue in their current role. Additionally, by pairing older workers with younger workers, the older contingent is exposed to new thinking and new technology in a nonthreatening manner and, as a by-product, will probably have greater enthusiasm and vitality.

At the risk of offending some because of a canine comparison, a frequent strategy recommended to owners of old dogs that are lethargic and no longer playful is to buy a new pup to keep the old dog company. In most cases, the result is that the older dog will start to romp and play and feel rejuvenated and more energetic, usually contributing to the extension of its life. In the human world, a similar feeling of rejuvenation and motivation for life can be seen when older people become grandparents. Similarly, younger workers can invigorate and stimulate older workers so that their overall attitude to work becomes more positive.

Coaching and mentoring programs are ideal ways for existing leaders to spend time with and effectively train their protégés. They can provide insight from past experiences as well as skill transference. A coach can assist a high-potential individual understand results-driven strategies to achieve the organization's objectives and goals, whereas a mentor is likely to assist by sharing experiences and offering insight and direction.

The following table distinguishes some of the characteristics between a mentor, a coach, and a manager who is "just" managing:

| Coach | Mentor | Manager |
| --- | --- | --- |
| **Has an individual perspective:** provides insight and perspective aligning an individual's developmental goals with those of the organization. | **Has a horizontal/systematic perspective:** provides insight and perspective that matches the flow of business across several different functions. | **Has a vertical perspective:** provides key insights and perspectives about the function or department they manage. |
| **Provides an external mirroring:** models effective two-way communication and feedback in order to improve the performance of a learner. | **Provides indirect authority:** not responsible for managing the performance of the learner. | **Provides direct authority:** responsible for the learner's performance and success on the job. |

(continued on next page)

| Coach | Mentor | Manager |
|---|---|---|
| **Advice to further development:** shares confidential and personal feedback but encourages learner to share development plans with others. | **Advice to broaden viewpoint:** allowed to share information to which the learner is seldom privy. | **Advice on performance improvement:** able to provide feedback on an ongoing basis so the learner knows how he or she is performing in relation to goals and objectives. |
| **Foster self-insight:** concerned with helping the learner grow through introspection and feedback from others. | **Foster self-responsibility:** concerned with helping the learner take charge of his or her own growth. | **Foster accountability:** responsible for monitoring performance and progress through appraisals and other formal systems. |
| **Concerns about personal growth:** concerned that the learner is successful at learning and becoming a more effective leader. | **Concerns about thinking:** ultimately concerned that the learner gains perspective and is successful at learning. | **Concerns with productivity:** concerned with the learner's success on the job. |

Beverly Kaye, (Section 5—Coaching & Mentoring), *Best Practices in Organization Development and Change.* Copyright © 2001 by Linkage Inc; This material is used by permission of John Wiley & Sons, Inc.

By combining high-potential individuals with experienced mentors and coaches within your organization, you provide targeted training that is greatly beneficial for future leadership as well as ensuring active involvement and retention of workers.

Sadly, due to recent trends towards retrenching older workers, many organizations have now lost large segments of their intellectual know-how and history. One company I worked with recently retrenched 75 percent of its most senior executives over a two-year period, then later regretted it when they realized they had lost the majority of their organization's history and "knowledge bank."

This can be seen as similar to the Stalinist purges of the 1930s where the upper echelons of the Red Army including generals, majors and colonels, were systematically killed or exiled by a jealous, insecure dictator. Historians agree that the great tragedy that overtook the Soviet Union in the early stages of WWII as the Nazis invaded was that it would have been less disastrous had the army not lost its most competent and able commanders.

The results of an unforeseen and unexpected challenge when the corporate memory of an organization has been "purged" through early retirement or forced retrenchment can be detrimental to future survival.

---

*Managers' fundamental task is providing the enabling conditions for people to lead the most enriching lives they can.*
Bill O'Brien, President of Hanover Insurance

---

# Third Age Career/ Life Planning

## Falling Off a Cliff

---

Inspired by the French term, "Troisiéme Age," the Third Age refers to the concept of lifelong learning, self-development, and fulfillment. It is a time of life characterized by vital living, freedom, personal growth and enrichment.

Thirdage Inc., San Francisco *www.thirdage.com*

---

Following a lifetime of work, the prospect of retirement can be challenging and unwelcome for many workers. Working towards voluntary retirement, people may work hard right up until their last day (perhaps even arriving late to their own retirement party), then find themselves unprepared to face the whole new world of retirement awaiting them because they've been too busy. For those older workers unexpectedly laid off from jobs, many discover the task of reentering the workforce after the age of 50 to be arduous and may decide to call it a day. They, therefore, embark upon an involuntary retirement they hadn't anticipated nor planned for, some years before they'd expected to retire.

Retirement following 30 or 40 years of hard work, possibly having experienced continual advancement and achievements throughout a career, can mean that suddenly familiar everyday activities and the way of life workers have known comes to an abrupt halt. It can be tantamount to climbing up a hill towards the sea—gradually climbing higher and higher until you reach the edge of the cliff, then plummet down the face of the cliff into the sea below.

Retirement has always been the ultimate goal for the American worker, the payoff for hectic years of work. People have seen it as a time when their lives become their own, when they can rest, travel and play at their own pace.

But more people are finding that traditional notions of old age and retirement are about as useful as an eight-track tape player. As people live longer and enter old age in better health, the generally accepted goals for this stage of life do not apply quite as universally—if they ever did.

Jocelyn Y. Stewart, "Retired No Longer Means No Work," *Los Angeles Times*, May 17, 2000. Copyright, 2000, Los Angeles Times. Reprinted with permission.

Many workers only discover afterwards, when it's too late, that retirement is not what they had envisaged and is not ideal for them. Where the main purpose and enjoyment in life has been involvement in work (no matter how junior or senior their role may have been), many find that, upon retirement, all that was familiar is gone and they are faced with the daunting question of "What will I do now?"

Of course, not everyone facing retirement is unprepared. However, in the work environment of the past decade, work has been all-encompassing for many of us. Because of long hours worked, a large proportion of workers have found themselves with limited quality time for family, friends, social pursuits, personal learning, hobbies, or sports. There has not been enough time for much of a life outside work, let alone converging into the years following working life, often referred to as "The Third Age."

These so called "third agers," a group encompassing people between 55 and 75, are interested in pursuing worthwhile projects such as advising fledgling businesses as well as donating hours to pursue personal passions or charity.

They are people like Fred Mandell, 61, of Needham. Mandell retired two years ago as head of American Express's investment company.

"I'm reluctant to say I'm retired, but, rather, that I am doing meaningful projects that keep me learning and growing," he said.

Laurie Geary, of Cambridge, who counseled executives for six years, has just hung out her retirement coaching shingle. She is now preparing workshops, she said, for people 55 years of age and older that will cover topics ranging from fulfilling work options to financial planning and fitness training.

"I want clients to realize that they can create, with planning, a whole new life," Geary said. "Too many people reach retirement age and say, 'Oops, what am I going to do now?'"

Segueing into another, very different stage of life is never easy. But it is a little easier when individuals are encouraged to follow through on their belief that "they can make a difference in what they do, often through new work, rather than golfing all day," said George Zeller, a senior employment specialist with the Jewish Vocational Service.

Davis Bushnell, "'Retirement' a Dirty Word for Many Older Workers," *The Boston Globe*, October 26, 2003.

---

If organizations encourage staff to continue working long hours in a high-pressured environment until retirement, it could potentially result in those individuals being too time restricted (and tired) to explore and pursue new activities and plan for an active retirement while still working. They may unintentionally condemn their employees to an early grave!

---

*The average life expectancy once a person retires with nothing to do is 5.7 years. Use it or lose it!*
Denis E. Waitley, Trainer, Author & Speaker

---

**Take Responsibility**

In these extremely tough and competitive times where the need to constantly strive to improve productivity and profitability is paramount, providing support to those approaching retirement is not always viewed as important or necessary. From my experience, when discussing the importance of assisting older workers with retirement plans, I have been alarmed by the looks of disbelief from those I'm presenting to and the common response of "what a waste of money!"

If organizations continue to neglect to assist their older workers to prepare and plan for retirement, the following negative effects could be incurred:

- Huge sickness expenses paid out to retirees linked to your medical benefits scheme.

- The disheartened response from other employees when they hear a former fellow worker has passed away shortly following retirement, possibly leading to loss of productivity and even their own early retirement.
- The detrimental impact on the organization's reputation.
- Workers planning retirement in company time, reducing productivity in the years leading up to retirement.

As we know, organizations are faced with the need to retain older workers longer due to the changing demographics within the workforce that are leading towards a future personnel deficiency. However, by encouraging older workers to work at full pace, it appears we are also unintentionally committing them to a shorter life.

---

*In his youth he spent his health to gain his wealth. In his aging he spent his wealth to gain his health.*
Anonymous

---

So many organizations recruit, induct, train, develop, promote, and then, at retirement, say good-bye and wipe their hands clean. Surely the responsibility of the employer should not end there. A corporation has, at the very least, a moral responsibility to assist their older workers to converge into retirement gradually and ensure that they plan for a long, active, and healthy retirement. If they do this, there are many benefits, including:

- Improved retention of workers of all ages by demonstrating commitment and support.
- Continued relationship to tap into intellectual knowledge of retirees when needed.
- Can rehire retirees in the future if required for short-term projects.
- Retirees become advocates of the organization, providing a good reputation, which can encourage others to seek employment with the corporation.

When we have grown used to a comfortable, routine, active existence, it can be extremely traumatic to be faced with the sudden onset of retirement. Suddenly, everything familiar is gone and major adjustment, choices, and decisions for the future need to be made. The experience can be felt as powerfully as the loss of a family member, a very serious and debilitating illness, or the end of a marriage. Although we go through a significant adjustment when we leave school to join the workforce for the first time, the adjustment is easier as we are young, adaptable, have a clearer vision of what to expect, and have not developed long-term habits and traits.

---

*Of all the traps and pitfalls in life, self-disesteem is the deadliest, and the hardest to overcome, for it is a pit designed and dug by our own hands, summed up in the phrase, "It's no use—I can't do it."*
Dr. Maxwell Maltz, Plastic Surgeon & Author

---

Demonstrating that your organization has a corporate conscience and implementing new strategies to assist employees to successfully make the transition into retirement will go a long way towards retaining staff and enhancing long-term profitability. Employers must take a benevolent approach and adopt a much greater level of sensitivity than that demonstrated in the majority of organizations over the past decade.

Unless there is a gradual transition towards the end of working life, the effect of such a dramatic change on an individual can be disastrous, just like falling off a cliff. How will you make sure that your employees are not just another potential statistic?

---

A serious and concentrated proactive and strategic role by human resource professionals will be necessary in the near future to maintain the knowledge base of their workforce in a competitive marketplace as the U.S. workforce ages.

HR should take a proactive role in developing benefits, retention and recruitment plans to attract retirees. After all, older workers have invaluable experiences other generations will not have for decades to come.

Society for Human Resource Management (SHRM) Study, June 22, 2003

---

## Phasing Down

Consideration must be given to what can be done to develop an environment of caring and assist older workers to achieve their desired work/life balance and support them to successfully make the transition into retirement. There are many low-cost methods that can contribute to creating a winning workplace and further enhance the profitability and reputation of the organization. The by-product of a proactive strategy can be a flexible workforce that can be adjusted up or down to meet the organization's needs in a nontraumatic way, depending on economic cycles and levels of demand.

---

Tom Griffiths retired as a telephone repairman at the end of his shift at the New York Stock Exchange one Friday last fall, "just as if I was going home to put my feet up on the porch," he said. Come Monday morning, though, he was back on the trading floor, fixing the same telephone lines, this time as a part-time worker, with his pension making up for the lost income.

"I was a little leery of accepting the offer to 'sort of' retire," admitted Mr. Griffiths, a 52-year-old Staten Island resident. But his employer offered cash bonuses to encourage older workers to exchange their job security and full-time compensation for a novel blend of work and retirement.

"I had a lot of bills," Mr. Griffiths said. "That was the driving force for me to take it." His incentives included $10,000, two years' salary and the chance to win future bonuses.

A number of large companies, including Avaya, Monsanto, PepsiCo and Lockheed Martin, are now finding ways to work around the legal obstacles and offer phased retirement.

Phased retirement can take many forms. At universities, it is used to clear out elderly tenured professors. But in the private sector, it is being promoted as a way to keep valued older workers in a tight labor market. Workers in their 50s who would otherwise take advantage of early retirement provisions in their pensions are offered the chance to work reduced hours and supplement their reduced incomes by tapping those pensions.

Other analysts wonder whether phased retirement is not just a new way of turning America's veteran employees into contingent workers, allowing corporations to subsidize their compensation costs by drawing down surplus pension assets.

"These are highly skilled, functional people, and they're being converted into part-time workers," said David C. Howard, a St. Louis lawyer who has represented former Monsanto workers in age-discrimination suits. "There's a whole across-the-board range of benefits that they're being excluded from. They're not getting merit-pay increases, advancements, promotions."

At Avaya, Michael A. Dennis, a vice president who negotiated his company's program, argued that phased retirement is a tool for preserving good jobs with benefits.

Employees in their mid-50s tend to present big liabilities, pension accruals, wages buoyed by seniority, rising health care costs. For those reasons, it was popular in the 1980s and 1990s to urge costly 55-year-olds to the door. Even after paying them cash incentives to retire, companies could replace them at lower cost with younger workers.

Now, though, after a decade of economic expansion, many companies find it hard to find skilled employees. Compensation consultants say retaining older employees is becoming more attractive, particularly as America's 76 million baby boomers age. The oldest boomers are turning 55 this year, an age at which most big companies with traditional pensions offer early retirement.

Worse, it has become apparent that when early retirees leave, they often take new jobs at other companies. And then they no longer look so expensive; many will work for wages only, because they already have health insurance and pensions.

Avaya's Mr. Dennis said this was on his mind as he drafted the company's phased-retirement plan. "We didn't want these folks retiring and going around and working for other companies that would be competing against us," he said. The breakthrough, he said, was finding a legal way of giving the older workers their pensions and keeping them in-house.

"Other companies are offering similar arrangements on a smaller scale," said Anna Rappaport, who surveyed 232 private and public-sector employers for the William M. Mercer consulting firm. She found that 36 percent were hiring back retirees as consultants and independent contractors without benefits, and 37 percent were hiring them back for part-time and temporary assignments.

Mary Williams Walsh, "No Time to Put Your Feet Up as Retirement Comes in Stages," *The New York Times*, April 15, 2001 Copyright © (2001) by The New York Times Co. Reprinted with permission.

---

Some contemporary organizations are now encouraging their future retirees to find meaningful use of their idle time and plan for their future while still working and earning money. It gives them a taste of what's to come and ensures that their intellectual knowledge and special skills are passed on to other workers before they depart, reducing the organization's vulnerability once they've left.

A successful way of doing this is to gradually phase down the hours worked by those workers approaching retirement. A very effective way to get workers to phase down and experience a taste of retirement in the last year of employment is to move them to working four days a week on full pay, then, for the last six months, work only three days a week, still on full pay. For the employees, it enables them to understand what it will be like to have idle time and encourages them to start planning for their retirement while still working.

Although there are costs involved in allowing people to work reduced hours on full pay during this final year, the resulting benefits of this forward-thinking approach far outweigh these costs. It will ensure the handing over of intellectual knowledge and special skills to other workers while still employed, therefore reducing dependence and vulnerability once they have retired.

So often, with the massive layoffs that have occurred over the last decade, organizations have lost their knowledge bank. Many organizations ignorantly accept skills walking out the door without being transferred to other workers, resulting in unnecessary downtime and loss of productivity and profitability.

---

Age discrimination is going to be banned from 2006 under an EU directive. Even before the necessary legislation takes effect in Britain, there are signs that employers' attitudes are changing. Several now recognize that they were too hasty in winnowing out the ranks of older workers who were the repository for much corporate memory and wisdom.

"Early Retirement? Don't Even Think About It," *The Economist*, March 23, 2002.
© 2002. The Economist Newspaper Ltd. All rights reserved. Reprinted with permission. www.economist.com

---

### Senior Sabotage

Employers need to take a proactive stance in assisting older workers plan for retirement; otherwise they could be prone to unintentional covert sabotage.

For many people, planning their own retirement can be an all-encompassing obsession for many years prior, counting down the days until they can put their feet up. However, due to any number of circumstances beyond their control, they could disappointingly find they need to put their retirement plans on hold and continue working.

Following the 2002—2003 U.S. stock exchange slump, many potential retirees found they were faced with a negative impact on their "401K" balances with less funds available for retirement than they had anticipated. Due to the unforeseen erosion of financial reserves experienced by "would be if they could be" retirees, visions of a condominium in the sun or an RV vacation around the country were put on hold as they found they had to extend their working life. Although these people continued to go to work and collect their pay, their hearts were no longer in the job role and productivity decreased, therefore costing employers money.

While older workers generally don't bear any malice or intend to create havoc and damage to their employers, if their level of productivity drops to a very low level, it can also have a negative impact on their fellow workers' morale, resulting in an unintentional "sabotage" to the employer.

---

77 percent of the companies Mercer surveyed have no formal programs in place to help employees gradually phase out of work. 65 percent said that doing so had not been a priority while 53 percent said the organization preferred to make such arrangements on an individual basis.

William M. Mercer and Company, 2001

---

## Third Age Transition

---

*Those who teach shall also learn and those who learn shall also teach.*
Peter Laslett, Founder of U3A (University of the Third Age), UK

---

The word *retirement* tends to have a stigma attached to it, whereby we envisage an "ending" rather than a "new beginning." I believe that referring to this phase of our lives as entering the Third Age to be a much more positive way to describe the end of full-time work and the commencement of a life specifically designed for a desired work/life balance. As described by the University of the Third Age, the Third Age denotes the age of active retirement, following the first age of childhood and schooling and the second age of vocational employment.

In order to effectively manage the transition of workers into their Third Age, ensuring optimum results for the employee and the organization, there are many important points to be considered:

1.  **Trust**

    An environment of trust is imperative when discussing retirement plans with employees. Communicating future aspirations and a desire to phase down to a shorter working week can be considered a bold and risky move. Many are afraid of voicing their intentions for fear that their name will be on the next list of layoffs should the organization find out their desires.

    Leaders must develop ways to boost trust within their organization so that workforce needs can be planned in an open environment and employees can discuss their career aspirations honestly.

2.  **Training**

    Courses and seminars on phasing down are a great way to be sure that the support available to them is communicated. There are seminars available that can be specifically tailored for an organization.

    DBM has a valuable "Retirement Success Program" (Copyright © 2002 DBM all rights reserved) that enables employees to develop a clear life plan for the future. Seminars are conducted over several days with ongoing interactive reviews occurring at specific times prior to retirement. Some key areas included in this important program include the following:

- Redefining and reorienting yourself
- Healthy resolution of attitude toward retirement
- Self-direction and empowerment
- Planning for good health
- Financial preparedness and planning
- Life satisfaction in work and retirement
- Life meaning and recapturing dreams
- Developing leisure interests
- Developing positive attitudes to change
- Family/relationship issues
- Developing your retirement success plan

This program is extremely interactive and encourages the participation and views of partners or spouses, ensuring retirement plans are developed to fit in with the home environment and not just specifically for the retiree.

### 3. Life or Emotional Planning

Regrettably, emotional issues are often ignored in planning for retirement. To have an active 20 to 30 years or more of retirement ahead, a clear life plan must be developed. By assisting workers to step into retirement confidently focused, you will provide them with a running and positive start for the next important chapter in their lives.

A former colleague of mine retired recently and, over his first breakfast as a retiree, asked his wife "So, what shall we do today?" She promptly responded with "I know what I'll be doing. I'm off to my meetings and will see you tonight!"

In households with two career breadwinners, one person may be experiencing significant change in his or her life due to retirement while the other continues with his or her usual routine. Alternatively, if there is only one breadwinner, the other partner may be involved in not-for-profit work, part-time work, sports, or other interests and pursuits that they wish to continue with. Often there is little discussion or planning with other household members, and the illusion of a relaxing retirement sharing time together can quickly turn into a big, dark abyss.

Developing a "life plan" involves taking time to identify interests, goals, passions, likes, dislikes, desires, hopes, and aspirations and preferably sharing them with those who will be closest to you during retirement. An individual must set milestones to achieve in order to ensure it is a living document.

From my many years in outplacement, I am all too familiar with people who don't give any consideration to their retirement plans. These people soon discover they are completely bewildered when it comes to knowing what to do with their free time and are at risk of having an unfulfilled (or shortened) life!

---

There is a growing recognition of the demoralizing effects of social isolation, particularly within the older sector of the community. Because it is largely invisible, it is an issue that until recently has been given scant attention. Being lonely is not something that many people are prepared to admit to; doing something about it seldom captures the imagination of mainstream society.

One organization that has been well aware of the impact of this situation is U3A, the University of the Third Age, an international movement designed to provide low-cost, lifelong learning opportunities for retired people in an informal atmosphere. Under one name or another, U3A now has several millions of members around the world. No prior qualifications are necessary and no degrees are awarded. Implicit in its philosophy is an understanding of the importance of the social interaction that it provides.

U3A Online is the outcome of an initiative of a group of U3A members. It was originally funded as a project for IYOP, the 1999 UN International Year of Older Persons. U3A Online has been developed to allow U3As to share ideas, resources and information through the Internet and to encourage older people to harness its seemingly unlimited educational potential. A centerpiece of the project is a program of special short courses, originally devised for older members of the community who are isolated, either geographically or through physical or social circumstances.

Dorothy Braxton, U3A Online, *www.u3aonline.org*

---

4. **Regular Reviews**

   Plans should be revisited on a regular basis (at least every six months) to assess whether a person is on track and whether modifications are required because of changing circumstances and new ideas. This way, the plan continues to be fine-tuned so that by the time retirement day is reached, it will be a matter of looking forward enthusiastically rather than clinging to the past.

5. **Five-Year Plan**

   Workers should commence planning for their retirement at least five years before the planned retirement date, to enable them to set down clear goals and implement their strategy while still working. The situation may be that, five years before retirement, work is all-encompassing. However, by developing a retirement/life plan, they can start identifying other areas of interest so that by the time they reach retirement, they have a portfolio of activities to occupy their days.

   As they step into retirement, they drop off the work activity (or possibly part of it and perhaps to continue to work for the organization part-time) and expand the other areas of interest. This provides a running and positive start for the next important stage of their lives.

British Telecom employees attend progressive preretire-
ment seminars three years prior to retirement. A year before
retirement, loved ones are also invited to participate in
life/plan development.

---

45+ workers want to remain engaged in the workforce well past traditional "retirement age," which long signaled the end of the working
life for so many people of previous generations. 69 percent say they
want to work into their retirement years. But they want to finish out
the latter stages of their careers in different roles and on different
terms than before. 34 percent say that during retirement they plan to
work on a part-time basis "for interest and enjoyment." Another 19
percent say they plan to work part-time for needed income, 10 percent plan to go into business for themselves and 6 percent intend to
work full-time in a new career altogether. These responses reflect a
relatively new, but increasingly common embrace among late-stage
workers of so-called "bridge jobs" that sustain them, offer them new
experiences and provide work life flexibility between careers or
before they leave the working world for good.

Staying Ahead of the Curve, The AARP Work and Career Study, A national study conducted for AARP by RoperASW, September 2002

---

6. **Support**

Ongoing support should be provided if required, such as
access to counseling and meeting with and learning from
those who have successfully made the transition into retirement. Highlighting role models within the organization will
help others to build confidence.

Support must also be provided to assist with regular
reviews of life plans to make certain that they are being
adhered to and not cast aside and considered too hard.

---

*HR professionals need to consider new performance incentives tailored to
older workers. Rather than cash, new incentives could include opportunities
to add vacation time, change work schedules and to assist in personal
development.*
Shari Fryer, Vice President, Marketing, DBM, USA

---

## 7. Financial Planning

Employers and governments around the world are working hard to address the issue of financial planning. While we are still a long way away from ensuring all employees have adequate savings to support their retirement years, many employees today have a greater awareness of savings plans for retirement, often through financial planning seminars.

Financial planning encourages employees to build up savings and manage their financial affairs effectively, and will assist workers to identify when they will be able to undertake retirement with the standard of living they desire.

Many of us have not clearly thought through the financial ramifications of living longer. There may be the need to work longer to build up required savings to fund the quality of life desired throughout a potentially longer retirement period than that of previous generations.

## Organizational Benefits

Assisting employees to make the transition into retirement or Third Age should not just be viewed as "a nice thing to do" and "a low-return investment" but rather a way to actually further enhance corporate profitability. Organizations that care about their employees' transition will reap the rewards, such as:

## 1. Motivation and Loyalty

There is a much greater chance that people will remain engaged and motivated through the remaining years of employment if they are positive about their future and respect that their employer is assisting them to establish a good foundation for a long and happy life. This, therefore, converts into more productive employees.

## 2. Focus

Rather than potential "silent sabotage," employees will focus more on their work responsibilities than spending time covertly planning their retirement and contributing less to the success of the organization.

## 3. Positive Message to Younger Workers

By demonstrating that the organization cares about its workers, it sends an extremely positive message to younger workers and therefore contributes to improved retention. Phased retirement demonstrates that the organization is a flexible employer.

4. **Ongoing Employment**

   An agreement for the employee to continue working beyond the proposed retirement date in a reduced capacity and less stressful role can be negotiated during retirement planning discussions. The majority of jobs today don't require brute strength, and older employees, with a wealth of knowledge, experience, and skills gained throughout their career, can make a very valuable ongoing contribution. It may even be possible for them to work remotely.

---

A survey of 232 large U.S. employers found that 55 percent have no specific goals for employing older workers. A relatively small percentage target retention efforts to workers with special expertise or key relationships (30 percent) or to workers with hard-to-replace skills (29 percent). Just 16 percent encourage all older workers to stay on.

William M. Mercer and Company, 2001

---

5. **Different Roles**

   The retirement planning process may provide the opportunity to offer different roles, such as reduced hours and responsibilities, to entice valued employees to remain associated with the organization beyond a planned retirement date.

6. **Ready Reserves/Mentors**

   By demonstrating support when an employee is approaching retirement, staff are more likely to be willing to return to the organization on a part-time or seasonal basis, perhaps in the role of mentor or consultant, should the need arise.

---

MITRE Corp, a 5,000 employee company that provides technology research and development centers for the Department of Defense, the Federal Aviation Administration and the Internal Revenue Service, based in Bedford, Mass., and McLean, Va., has been proactive in considering the impact of an aging workforce. The average age of MITRE's employees is about 45—more than ten years above the national median age.

MITRE enables older employees to stay in the workforce not only through phased retirement, part-time work and sabbaticals but also through its "Reserves at the Ready" program. The program allows employees with at least ten years' of company service to become part-time on-call employees, staffing projects throughout the corporation.

This enables older employees to mentor younger workers and pass along technical expertise and in-depth knowledge of agencies involved with MITRE. Reserves include those experienced in technical, administrative and secretarial positions. Bill Albright, director of quality of work life and benefits, says MITRE finds its older workers to be creative and productive—"great contributors." MITRE has received an award from AARP for exemplary practices toward older workers.

Alison Stein Wellner, *HR Magazine*, March 2002

---

7. **Cost Saving**

   When analyzing costs involved with replacing someone who exits the organization, such as recruitment fees, induction, time spent training and developing, and the risk associated with a new recruit (as it is often not possible for three to six months to determine whether someone's aptitude, abilities, and potential fits with organizational objectives), the net result is a very significant sum. Many estimate the cost of replacing someone to be equivalent to approximately six to nine months' salary. Based on this calculation, it may be more cost-effective to retain an employee longer if possible.

8. **Minimize Impact**

   If retirement becomes involuntary due to a necessary downsizing that occurs prior to a planned retirement date, a person will already be prepared for life beyond the organization and will be able to speed up his or her transition into a new life. The trauma normally associated with an unexpected loss of a job can be minimized from that of what it would have been if there had been no retirement planning offered.

   Negative fallout that usually occurs from a downsizing can be reduced, as the remaining employees feel the organization has assisted the person leaving with their transition, therefore reducing the impact on morale and productivity.

---

*We do not stop playing because we grow old; we grow old because we stop playing.*
Anonymous

---

# The Bell Curve and Retractable Retirement

## Bell Curve Solution

The concept of a career plan whereby an employee is able to move up the corporate ladder and then, at a time of his or her choosing, phase down to fewer responsibilities is known as a "bell curve" career. Following the curve of the bell, people commence working life in a junior role, gradually working their way up to a point where they decide they no longer wish to attain further promotion and choose to gradually reduce their responsibilities along the path to ultimate retirement. Many workers reach a point in their career where they desire a more flexible role and may choose to reject promotion (and even accept demotion) in order to achieve less stress and fewer working hours, even if it means less money and status.

Phasing down the right side of the bell curve (after climbing up the left side) makes sense for the corporation as well as the individual. It encourages valuable employees to remain with the company and continue to be engaged and motivated and, at the same time, plan to achieve their work/life balance. This concept can be applied successfully to all workers, no matter what their responsibilities are, within the organization.

Business leaders may see people who express their intention to step down from their current level of responsibility as those who have lost their drive and commitment to the organization. However, by creating an environment of open trust and communication, employees will be able to share with their employer their desired planned for work/life balance, and may avoid the need to leave the organization to achieve their goals.

Many people are inclined to regularly reconsider what is important in their lives in order to achieve a work/life balance.

This may be prompted at various ages for various reasons, such as personal issues, financial responsibilities, health, tragic world events, or any number of alternative reasons. In order to achieve the best results, it makes sense to strive to ensure that employees' personal goals are aligned with organizational goals to have a fully productive workforce.

---

The expectations of older persons and the economic needs of society demand that older persons be able to participate in the economic, political, social and cultural life of their societies. Older persons should have the opportunity to work for as long as they wish and are able to, in satisfying and productive work, continuing to have access to education and training programs. The empowerment of older persons, and the promotion of their full participation, are essential elements for active aging.

Political Declaration, Second World Assembly on Aging, United Nations, Madrid, May 2002

---

## Retractable Retirement

---

**retire** *(vb)*
*To give up or to cause (a person) to give up his work, esp. on reaching a pensionable age.*
*To go away as into seclusion, for recuperation*
*To recede or disappear ...*
Collins Dictionary

---

How often have you heard a comment such as: "It's such a shame Mary's retired. We sure could use her knowledge and experience with this problem!" But, of course, no one actually thinks to phone Mary to discover she would gladly return to the organization in an instant to help out. Instead, we assume that because someone's retired, they have now left for another planet and are no longer accessible.

Here's something you may not realize: Retirement doesn't have to be forever. Retirees are allowed to change their minds. They can return to the workforce if that is their choice for securing a better life or if an opportunity is presented to them that provides them with their desired work/life balance.

> Realize that retirement is a relatively new concept in human evolution. A few generations ago, before social security and full-time leisure became culturally embedded as the "norm," elders remained productive members of society, relied upon for their insight, wisdom and skills.
>
> Top Ten Ways to Reinvent Retirement, 2 Young 2 Retire™, *www.2young2retire.com*

Many people believe retirement to be the ultimate reward for working hard over the years, to finally reach the point in their lives where they can relax and occupy their time as they choose. But, unfortunately, many retirees find themselves confronted by a super-abundance of free time and frustration. Reality does not always match the dream.

I know of a man who couldn't wait to replace the day-to-day stress of working life to play golf at every available moment. He retired as soon as he reached age 55. Today, regrettably, six years into retirement, he finds that he can't afford to play golf as regularly as he had hoped. Perhaps if he chose to return to work he could put himself in a stronger financial position and continue to play his beloved golf.

> *It is better to wear out than to rust out.*
> Anonymous

Although there are usually many developments and changes in the world of work between the time someone retires and the time they choose to return to work, this can be overcome by assigning suitable training and understanding both the organization's and the individual's needs.

After several retirement years of waking up when they feel like it and occupying their time each day with activities they have chosen, it may take a little adjustment and discipline to fall back into a work routine. However, if these people choose to reenter the workforce, they will undoubtedly be prepared to face the challenges involved and gain workplace confidence quickly, in preference to having an unfulfilling life in retirement. Also, many people maintain business interests and stay up-to-date with workplace trends in retirement, therefore making it an easier transition to slip back into working life.

Outsourcing has created a range of new opportunities for people to return to the workplace in a part-time capacity, such as working as contractors or consultants. This situation offers older workers the opportunity to gain enjoyment and stimulation from reentering the workforce and earning additional income to support their desired lifestyle.

Because we are rapidly evolving into a "24/7" way of work, more and more organizations are offering round-the-clock service thereby creating many opportunities for older workers to fill the needs of newly created roles.

It also allows them to retain adequate leisure time to pursue "nonwork" priorities and, most importantly, have fun with their life.

---

*Retirement takes all the fun out of Saturdays.*
Anonymous

---

### Continuing a Flexible Relationship

With pressure mounting on organizations to retain employees and boost productivity, it is necessary to recognize the value of continuing a successful flexible employment relationship with older workers both before and after retirement. The benefits of an ongoing flexible relationship include:

- Can retain older workers following retirement, either in a reduced capacity or to continue in full-time employment (if it is an attractive option for both parties).
- The opportunity to use older workers as mentors for younger workers ensures that Gen X and Gen Y employees learn skills faster than may have been otherwise possible.

---

*Age should not have its face lifted, but it should rather teach the world to admire wrinkles as the etchings of experience and the firm line of character.*
Ralph B. Perry, Philosopher

---

- Transferring to a part-time role rather than leaving altogether provides an orderly transference of intellectual knowledge to other employees, particularly if a clear plan is adopted.

- The chances of employees having a longer life after they leave the service of your organization are greatly improved. An older employee with great experience and skills can make a very valuable ongoing contribution.

It is interesting to note, through British Telecom's flexible employment strategy allowing many employees to work from home, that products created to assist staff to work remotely have now been developed into new products targeted at the significant home-office market.

---

*It gives me great pleasure to converse with the aged. They have been over the road that all of us must travel and know where it is rough and difficult and where it is level and easy.*
Plato, Greek Philosopher

---

The benefits to older workers wishing to maintain an association with their organization following retirement include:

- They can continue to earn money to fund retirement. With longer life expectancy, many retirees are realizing that they may not have adequate savings to fund the quality of life they wish to have in a potentially much longer retirement.
- They can achieve a work and leisure balance by working part-time, on a seasonal basis, or on special projects, creating the perfect transition into retirement and avoiding future shock.
- They can feel like they are still making a contribution and have a sense of achievement and belonging.
- They can keep their mind stimulated to a greater degree.

---

55 percent of workers 45+ said they will continue to work only because of the money. 76 percent say money is one of the major reasons, while 67 percent say saving for retirement was a motive. 80 percent of 45+ workers believe that most people can't afford to retire altogether.

Staying Ahead of the Curve, The AARP Work and Career Study, A national study conducted for AARP by RoperASW, September 2002

---

When we look at the majority of job roles, we realize that very rarely do we spend more than 10 or 20 percent of our time on strategic activities, even if we're the CEO. The majority of our time is devoted to operational, tactical, administrative, or processing work. Someone who phases down to take on a part-time role may be ideal to provide strategic input, with operational-type work being delegated to a lower-cost employee, which will provide additional return to the organization.

We are often faced with difficulties in recruiting trained and experienced workers to capitalize on opportunities when faced with a significant surge in demand. By having employees phase into retirement, possibly continuing to work part-time, it is always possible to negotiate with the employee to return and work longer hours, perhaps even full-time for a period, to assist as necessary. Maintaining a good relationship with older workers increases their willingness to assist. You will have access to a significant pool of knowledge from which to rehire when necessary. Rehired employees can help out with:

- Seasonal roles
- Filling in when holidays are taken
- Covering for those on sick leave
- Assisting with a new project
- Relocating premises
- Special projects
- Troubleshooting
- Mentoring
- Coaching
- Job Sharing
- On-call work
- Consulting

By taking the bell curve approach, retirement plans may be reconsidered. Workers who may have once desired retirement at 50, 55, or 60 may continue their association in a part-time role for many years beyond 60. You will be able to create the potential for a large contingent workforce for many years to come, enabling you to address future increases in demand and become a winning workplace.

---

*The most important pattern of progress now emerging is an unmistakable trend towards healthier, longer life.*
1998 World Health Report, The World Health Organization

---

## They Don't Retire Them, They Hire Them

The following *Workforce Management* article by Joe Mullich highlights the importance of employing older workers and details
some of the creative approaches by organizations faced with skills
shortages to retain and reemploy older workers.

---

After the September 11 twin towers tragedy, the FBI confronted an
unusual problem in trying to launch a worldwide terrorism investigation:
inexperience. More than 40 percent of the 11,400 FBI agents around
the world had five or less years on the job. While it began a massive
campaign to hire new agents, the FBI turned to another source for the
immediate investigation. The agency hired dozens of its retired agents
on a contract basis as intelligence analysts and evidence examiners.

The retired agents couldn't carry guns, and they were classified as
"temporary" employees so as not to disrupt their pension benefits.
However, experts say, their abilities were sorely needed. A congres-
sional committee looking into intelligence failures linked to September 11
cited a lack of analytical skills as perhaps the FBI's greatest weakness.
According to the committee, the agency had failed to appreciate the
importance of several pieces of information related to possible terrorist
activity just before the attacks. Ironically, experts say, the FBI contributed
to this problem with its mandatory retirement age of 57, which forced
many of its most experienced analysts out of work. "They inadvertently
created a brain drain," says Robert F. Morison, director of research for
the Concours Group, a consulting firm in Kingwood, Texas.

While the FBI's lack of experienced workers is particularly dramatic, this "brain drain" mirrors the situation that companies and
organizations throughout the country will soon face. 11,000 Americans
turn 50 every day, the Department of Labor reports. The pending
retirements of baby boomers will strip the workforce of massive numbers of skilled workers for whom, as the FBI found, there are no quick-
and-easy replacements. This loss of workers "could put whole businesses in jeopardy," says Jane Paradiso, national practice leader of
workforce planning at Watson Wyatt Worldwide in Washington, D.C.

In many cases, companies that are just beginning to deal with this
problem have found the same solution as the FBI. Retired and older
employees, who were often brushed aside by hiring managers in the past
decade's obsession with youth, could be the solution to the approaching
worker shortage. The AARP recently completed a nationwide survey
of 2,001 people between the ages of 50 and 70, asking about their
views on retirement. 63 percent said they plan to work at least part-
time in retirement; five percent said they plan to never retire, some

because they like working, others because they need the money to replace lost retirement savings. Experts say this new older workforce will make it necessary for companies to rethink their approach on everything from recruitment and training to benefits and providing new challenges.

Steve Wing, director of government programs for the CVS drugstore chain, isn't given to hyperbole, but when asked about the importance of older workers to his company, he says, "Without older workers, we wouldn't have a company." CVS, anticipating the changes in workforce demographics, began specifically recruiting workers past the half-century mark a decade ago. In 1992, seven percent of its 10,000 employees were over 55. At that time, the company did a study of its older workers and made some surprising discoveries. Older workers, it turned out, were much less likely to call in sick than their younger colleagues. When CVS looked closely at the roles that older workers were performing, misconceptions about their physical and mental capacities were also bashed: 70-year-olds were still lifting heavy boxes; 90-year-olds held demanding managerial positions.

In the past ten years, through heavy recruiting efforts, CVS has more than doubled its over-55 workforce, which now represents 16 percent of the company. The effort started slowly. Initially, CVS representatives went to senior centers and pitched the company as a great place for older workers. "Of the 100 people who came to the presentation, only ten wanted to work, but those were the ten we wanted," Wing says.

At first, older workers were separated into their own training programs. CVS, which maintains six learning centers around the country, found that the older workers took longer to grasp certain things, such as technology. Over time, though, CVS learned that older workers needed less training in other areas, including customer service. "Many older people have a work ethic and sense of civility that the younger generation has not learned yet," Wing says.

CVS eventually merged the training groups, realizing that the different generations could learn from one another and would be working together eventually anyway. "The older people provided a great example of work ethic and customer service for the young people," Wing says. "The younger people help revitalize the older workers and give them enthusiasm for work."

## Supervising your grandparents

A large older workforce brings special challenges. Some CVS managers were uncomfortable supervising employees who were old enough to be their parents or grandparents. "At first, some of the younger managers were concerned that these older workers might try to take their jobs, but we found that many of the older workers had already done the management thing and now just wanted to work," Wing says.

CVS hired a consultant to provide training to head off intergenerational misunderstandings, such as an older worker who preferred to be called Mister instead of Pops by his younger colleagues. Most of the skills the consultant preached were simply about showing respect, and applicable to anyone, so CVS incorporated this perspective into its general training program.

Today, CVS has linked its recruitment efforts with the AARP and the National Council on the Aging, a national training and employment services organization for mature workers based in Washington, D.C. CVS tries to match the number of older workers in each of its stores to the demographics of the particular community the store serves. As its customer base ages, CVS finds, more customers want to see older workers.

"Some retailers use older workers just as greeters, but we employ them throughout the organization in all sorts of roles," Wing says. "We have workers into their 70s, and some in their 90s, who are not just holding down entry-level jobs."

CVS often turns to older workers to fill positions that require high amounts of organization and discipline. For instance, older workers are often put in charge of the greeting-card sections, which are key profit centers for which inventory must be selected and ordered wisely "so that all the dollars don't end up being tied up in drawers," Wing says. For hard-to-fill pharmacist-support positions, the company tries to recruit older workers with a medical background, such as retired nurses. Like other companies, CVS finds that filling positions often means looking for skills rather than specific experience. Recently, for example, CVS hired an older former information technology manager to run one of its stores. "We didn't have an IT position in his area," Wing says. "He didn't have any retail experience, but that's something we can teach. The other skills he had, like knowing how to work with people and get things done, take years to develop."

Attributes of loyalty and dedication, which CVS's survey connected with older workers a decade ago, still hold true today. Wing likes to tell the story of an 80-year-old pharmacy technician who has been with the company for 60 years and now works in a CVS store in Zanesville, Ohio. During a savage snowstorm last year, the technician was the only one who made it to work. "She called her manager and said, 'Where is everybody?'"

## Looking for flexibility

Noting the aging population, consultant Paradiso says, "What Florida looks like today, the United States will soon look like." David Fleming already knows what it's like to recruit workers in a geographic region with an older population. He heads the human resources department at Brethren Village, a continuing-care retirement community in Lancaster, Pennsylvania. Because Lancaster is an older area, so is Brethren's workforce: 34 percent of its workers (182 out of 529) are over age 50. Fleming goes to senior job fairs, where he stresses the many job attributes at Brethren that surveys show are particularly important to older workers.

For one thing, Brethren provides flexible schedules. If workers want to spend the winter in Florida, Brethren will be happy to employ them during the warmer months. Knowing that health insurance can be a hot-button topic for older workers, Brethren gives health-care coverage year-round to part-time workers.

According to surveys by Watson Wyatt and others, many older workers, particularly those who opt for part-time work, look for companies that will provide "bridge" medical coverage until Medicare kicks in. 17 percent of the AARP survey respondents said "a need for health benefits" was a key reason they would work during retirement. Giving full medical benefits to older workers who decide to go part-time, experts say, can be an effective way to hang on to skilled employees, and can be cheaper than bringing in new workers who must be trained.

Beyond this, Brethren stresses the training that workers receive. Brethren has difficulty finding enough workers in key areas like the facilities maintenance department, so it looks for ways to help workers stretch their skills. If the department needs to put up wallpaper but can find only painters, it will hire them and send them to wallpapering classes or bring in a trainer. "When our older workers talk to their friends at church and other places, they are always impressed by the amount of training we give them," Fleming says. "The word spreads that this is a good place for senior workers, and the idea of working here catches fire."

In the AARP survey, respondents were asked to rate the importance of various attributes of the jobs they hold or plan to hold in retirement. Factors that contributed to a life/work balance and allowed workers to grow and learn new skills were deemed "very important" by half of those polled. An important aspect of attracting and retaining older workers is offering them new roles and responsibilities, so they have a continuing sense of self-discovery. However, in a survey of 150 HR executives conducted by the Conference Board last year, two-thirds of the respondents said they don't offer training for mature workers as an incentive to upgrade skills. Companies like Brethren that do this have an edge in tapping into the older workforce.

## Easing back into work

Partly because of the influx of older workers, Brethren instituted a more aggressive mentoring program for new hires three years ago. Fleming found that after the normal orientation, new hires often had many questions, especially older employees who had been lured out of retirement and had not been in the workforce for many years.

In the mentoring program, new employees meet daily with an appointed "buddy" to help them adjust to the workplace. This is in addition to the interaction the new employees have with their own supervisor. "It reassures individuals reentering the workforce that they made the right decision to come to Brethren," Fleming says. "It shows that we listen and care about our workers."

St. Mary's Medical Center, in Huntington, West Virginia, provides a similar kind of assurance to older workers and others that it lures out of retirement. Like the rest of the health-care industry, St. Mary's faces a critical shortage of nurses. Two years ago, St. Mary's began looking beyond nursing-school graduates and other traditional sources to bolster its depleted ranks. The medical center sent letters to older alumni of a local nursing school and its own retiree club, asking if they wanted to return to work.

Understandably, some of the returning St. Mary's nurses, who had been retired for up to 20 years, were concerned about dealing with new technology and other changes in the fast-paced medical field. The re-entry program helped nurses who had let their licenses lapse get recertified. More important, the nurses were at first assigned to less demanding tasks. They handled the initial assessment of patients and did things like change IV tubing, rather than provide intensive patient care. After six months or so, some of those nurses opted to move into more demanding roles.

Over the past two years, the re-entry program has added 18 nurses to St. Mary's 600-person nursing staff. "That may not sound like a lot, but when you are trying to plug a hole in a middle shift, those nurses are heaven-sent," says Jennifer Gore, a nurse recruiter at St. Mary's. And since nursing positions make up 75 percent of all hospital vacancies nationwide, there are a lot of holes to fill.

## Age-friendly workplace

Experts agree that many older people will not apply for positions because they think they don't have a chance of being hired, or won't be treated well if they are. Companies that bend over backward to correct these misconceptions have a better chance of tapping into the older workforce. Volkswagen of America Inc. has never actively recruited older workers, but the average age of its workforce is 44.

Understandably, the carmaker has put a lot of effort into creating an "age-friendly" workforce.

One way that Volkswagen achieves this is by asking older workers for suggestions on how to avoid age barriers, a simple technique that companies often overlook. In addition, the company's Diversity Committee includes a number of older managers who help other managers become more sensitive to older workers' needs.

Those efforts are backed up with action. Older workers are encouraged to go back to school, take part in professional organizations and serve as mentors to younger colleagues. In the company's mentoring program, the more seasoned workers spend three to four hours a month with high-potential employees who have less experience. Stephen Stephens, Volkswagen's human resources leader, says that the relationship is good for the employees and the company.

Baptist Health South Florida, a nonprofit health-care provider, also makes sure that its older workers are treated fairly. Any action that might be detrimental to a worker with 15 years or more of service, such as a demotion, pay cut or job elimination, must be approved by a three-person committee consisting of Baptist's president, the head of human resources and the vice president in charge of the workers' department. The human resources department also has two "inside moves" representatives who help workers to change jobs internally, such as transferring to positions that are less physically demanding and require less lifting, says Carl Gustafson, Baptist's corporate vice president of human resources.

The company doesn't do all this out of compassion or kindness. About 24 percent of its 10,000 workers are over age 50. "We need these workers," Gustafson says. "So we need to do whatever it takes to keep them."

Joe Mullich, "They Don't Retire Them, They Hire Them," *Workforce Management*, December 2003, pp. 49–54

# 14

# Voyage Of Discovery

## Investigate the Future

---

*Success occurs when opportunity meets preparation.*
Anonymous

---

The questions contained in this chapter are designed to assist you, as a business leader or human resource professional, to review and investigate the current environment in which your employees work. These questions will help identify how well prepared you are for the forthcoming demographic changes and help you to optimize the potential within your organization.

I know answering questions can be tedious, however, think of the questions that follow as thought prompters. These investigative questions, which have proved extremely valuable when planning future personnel needs, are designed and developed from many hundreds of hours interviewing management of diverse corporations around the world and extensive interaction with HR professionals and are linked to the areas covered within this book so far.

No doubt you have a busy schedule, but taking the time to consider and address some of these questions will highlight what planning is necessary now to ensure future success. These questions should be revisited regularly and treated as a dynamic process. Perhaps you might wish to tackle the following questions together with your management team so that no bases are missed when planning for the future. You may identify with one or more subsection in particular and choose to focus on that group of questions in more detail.

This is a vital process of discovery, not only from an organizational overview, but also from a personal perspective. It will stimulate thinking about your organizational setup, the people within it, the role you play, the changes taking place, and the action that must be taken to achieve ongoing profitability and prosperity.

While some questions may not apply and others may seem superfluous and mundane, they have been included for good reason. I have often discovered many of the simple, yet important, questions are so often and easily overlooked. If you believe a particular question is not entirely relevant to your organization, that's fine. But at least review and consider all questions. By answering honestly, the steps and changes required to retain and motivate good people within your organization should become clear.

## Questions

---

*It's not the strongest nor most intelligent of the species that survive; it is the one most adaptable to change.*
Charles Darwin, British Scientist

---

## DEMOGRAPHIC MIX

### Workplace Demographics

- How many people do you employ?
- How many employees do you have under 35?
- How many employees do you have between 36 and 50?
- How many employees do you have over 50?
- How many employees do you have over 65?
- How many employees will be eligible for retirement over the next five years?
- What will be the impact of not having sufficient workers to achieve optimum productivity in the future?
- What is your current staff turnover? Has it increased or decreased over the last two years?
- What is the demographic shift that is occurring in the labor force in your region?

### Multigenerational Mix

- What is your multigenerational mix within the workplace?
- What impact do you foresee from an aging workforce?
- What are the various generational mindsets within the workplace?

- Do you have significant diversity with your workforce? How is this respected?
- How do you ensure that the diversity of your workforce matches the diversity of your customer base?

## Older Workers

- What percentage of your employees would you classify as older workers?
- Do you believe older workers have significant strengths and, if so, what are they?
- Do you offer phase-down options for the older members of your workforce?
- If so, what phase-down options do you offer?
- If not, do you believe older workers would respond positively to them, and how would it impact on your business operations?
- What support is offered for transition into retirement?
- If any support is offered, how long before a retirement date is it implemented?
- Do you maintain contact with people following retirement so you can access them in periods of staff shortages?
- Would you rehire an older worker, either full-time or part-time?
- Do you wish to retain older workers and, if so, why?
- How do you create an environment so that older workers can act as mentors within the workplace?

## Younger Workers

- What are the strengths of the younger workers in your workforce?
- What are their weaknesses, and have they been addressed?
- Have you identified those with high potential?
- What strategies have you implemented to develop high potentials?
- What retention strategies do you have in place for these people, and are they working?
- How do you create a flexible work environment for younger workers?

# PERFORMANCE

## Performance Management

- What performance management systems do you have in place?
- Are you familiar with the abilities, experience, and potential of your employees?
- How do you create an open environment to make sure you are confidently aware of the career goals of each employee?
- How do you ensure that personal goals of employees and organization goals are aligned?
- Does your leadership team meet with employees individually to discuss their personal goals and aspirations?
- Do you monitor and recognize achievements of personnel? Do you praise them?
- How often do you conduct performance reviews and provide honest feedback to employees?
- Are budgets and goals developed by the employees and passed up, or developed at the top level and pushed down? Do people own their budgets?

---

*The unexamined life is not worth living.*
Socrates, Greek Philosopher

---

## Recognition and Rewards

- How do you define a good worker? Are there clear performance goals?
- How do you recognize and reward your hardworking employees who exceed their job requirements?
- Can you give an example of a particular employee who stands above the rest and why? How have you recognized that person?
- Are you able to articulate what personal qualities you consider necessary for someone to succeed within your organization?
- Do you recognize achievements that help revenue growth or save costs?
- Do you recognize and reward creativity and initiative?
- Do you have a documented reward program in place, and are the employees aware of it?

- What additional enticements (monetary and/or nonmonetary) do you provide for workers to remain with your organization?

## Training and Development

- Do you provide job-specific training to all workers?
- Do you invest in the development of your workers over 50?
- How do you undertake a training-needs analysis?
- Do you have a training budget each year?
- How has the organization made a commitment to train and develop people to make certain that they are fully equipped to perform their job roles effectively?
- Do you believe you are a "learning organization"?
- How do you encourage and monitor skill development?
- Do you provide personal growth opportunities on a consistent and regular basis?
- Will the organization invest consistently in developing people of all ages?
- How do you monitor and measure the effectiveness of training initiatives?
- Is anyone (including you) exempt from attending regular training?
- Are your own skills up-to-date? How could they be improved?
- Do you provide time each year for employees to undertake adequate training (including yourself)?

## Recruitment

- Can you clearly identify the qualities and skills you need when hiring?
- Do you have a well-structured and thorough process to recruit people?
- Will you be able to replace most of those retiring in future years by way of internal appointments?
- Do you rehire people who have formerly worked with your organization? If not, why not?
- Do you find it difficult or easy to recruit people with the right skills that fit with your workplace culture?
- Do you focus on recognizing and developing talent from within or primarily recruit externally?
- Do you believe there is potential to undertake more internal promotions?

- Have you clearly defined the personal qualities you seek when recruiting?
- When recruiting, how well do candidates regard your organization compared to competitors?

## LEADERSHIP

### Dealing with Change

- Are your workers used to adapting to change and happy to do so?
- How do you communicate a change event? Is it by email?
- How have you measured the profit impact of change events in the past?
- How could you have managed change better?
- How do you address the emotional and psychological impacts of change?
- How do you allocate responsibility to ensure that a change event occurs with minimum impact?
- How do you keep your finger on the pulse and remain up to date with the changing world of work? When did YOU last undertake training?

### Workplace Communication

- Who does your staff turn to if they have concerns and important issues to discuss?
- With important information, do you prefer to communicate by phone, email, or by speaking to people in person? Which form of communication do you believe to be most effective?
- How do you encourage intergenerational communication?
- Do you encourage interdepartmental communication or prefer people to work in "silos"?
- Do you share financial details with all employees? If not, why not?
- How do you communicate organizational goals, achievements, values, challenges, and changes to employees?
- How do you ensure effective communication among workers at all levels?
- How do you encourage communication upwards from all levels of employees?
- Do you communicate your values to all workers?

*It's best to feed troops on victory.*
General John Monash, Australian Military Leader

## Problem Solving

- Do you encourage risk taking?
- Do you encourage creative thinking and brainstorming?
- How do you deal with mistakes?
- Do you create a positive learning environment?
- Do you set realistic tasks for employees and encourage them to solve them?

## People Management

- Do you hold regular team meetings to share achievements, discuss performance, and set goals?
- Do you encourage positive competition among workers?
- How do you encourage employees to feel empowered and in control of their own careers and job roles?
- Are you genuinely empathetic to the wants and needs of employees? How do you create an environment to find out what they really think?
- How do you actively encourage teamwork within the workplace?
- Are your employees passionate about their duties and enjoy coming to work each day?
- How do you make sure that your employees feel valued and recognized within the organization?
- Do you encourage employees to make decisions and support their actions?
- Do you encourage creative problem solving and create an appropriate environment to do so?
- Are you aware of your employees' backgrounds, experience, skills, and knowledge?
- Is each manager respected by his or her team of workers? Do you make an effort to find out accurately?
- Do you have key members involved in planning?
- How do you make sure that your employees stay focused on goals?

- How do you actively combine workers of different age groups?

## Future Leadership

- Who are the key people you have identified who are suitable for future leadership within your workplace?
- How do you plan to retain your potential future leaders and keep them motivated?
- How will you recruit future leaders if an internal appointment is not possible?
- Have you identified all high-potential employees worthy of future promotion?
- Do you have older workers who can support the development of people into leadership roles in the capacity of mentor or coach?

## Succession Planning

- Do you have a clear succession plan in place for all management and supervisory roles within the organization?
- How many people will be eligible to retire over the next five years?
- Are you developing key people so that they are fully equipped to take on the increased responsibilities?
- How often do you revisit the succession plan to ensure that it is always up to date?
- Do key people have career development plans in place that they have signed off on?

---

*Man's Desires are limited by his Perceptions; none can desire what he has not perceived.*
William Blake, British Poet

---

## Dealing with Difficult People

- How do you address issues of disrespect within the workplace?
- Can you cite examples of dealing with problem people and achieving a positive outcome?

- How do you discipline someone who doesn't have the best interests of the organization at heart and still retain and motivate that person?
- How do you address a member of staff who has the wrong attitude, which may lead to a detrimental impact on the success of the organization?
- How do you respond to gossip within the workplace, and how can you minimize it?

---

The oyster needs the speck of sand to irritate it just enough to produce the beauty and wonder of a pearl. Likewise, feelings of disharmony act as the emotional "sand" required for change.

Des Coroy, *Communicate or Disintegrate,* The Oracle Press, 2002

---

## Leadership and Management Style

- Do you focus more on long-term planning or short-term planning?
- Do you communicate effectively at all levels within the organization? What is your preferred method of communication, and is it effective?
- How do you make sure that your employees understand your credibility and respect you as their leader?
- What do you see as your strengths when it comes to leadership and people management?
- How can you improve your ability to deal with people effectively?
- What are your biggest weaknesses when it comes to managing people? Have you asked other people for their feedback?
- How do you respond to problems—calmly or aggressively?
- Do you consider yourself to be a good listener?
- What do you consider to be the reasons you have achieved personal success within your organization so far?
- Are you an effective public speaker who can convey messages effectively?
- Do you think it is necessary to undertake training to improve your ability to communicate in a positive manner?
- How do you align personal goals of your employees with corporate goals in a cooperative and flexible way?

# WORK/LIFE BALANCE

## Flexibility

- Do you offer flexible career plans for younger and older workers to address their changing needs and desires?
- Do you allow job sharing at senior and/or junior levels?
- Do you allow valuable employees to work reduced hours and accept reduced responsibilities?
- Do you allow people to work remotely, either full-time or part-time, depending on their job role?
- How do you create an environment for employees to talk openly about their desired levels of flexibility and plan accordingly?
- Are there any other areas of flexibility that you provide?

## Personal Time

- How do you actively encourage your employees to achieve a healthy work/life balance?
- Do you make allowances for people who are experiencing difficulties outside of work?
- Do you care whether your employees are leading healthy lives outside the workplace?
- Do you offer flexible work hours and responsibilities when possible?
- What initiatives and training do you have in place to encourage employees to have a good work/life balance?
- Do you have a good work/life balance, and are you happy?

---

*If you enjoy what you do, you will never work another day in your life.*
Confucius, Chinese Philosopher

---

## Social Activity

- Do you encourage social get-togethers of employees?
- Do you encourage partners and families of employees to attend organizational business and social functions? Should you?
- Are social functions looked forward to or perceived as a burden?

- Do you conduct group meetings outside the work environment?
- Do you believe social activities linked with the workplace are good or unimportant? Do they help productivity?

---

*When one door closes, another opens; but we often look so regretfully upon the closed door, that we do not see the one which has opened for us.*
Alexander Graham Bell, Inventor

---

## ORGANIZATIONAL CULTURE

### Work Environment

- What have you implemented to ensure a happy and productive work environment?
- Do you allow personal expression in dress in the workplace? Is there flexibility?
- Does the environment suit those who work within it?
- Is your technology up-to-date? How do you know?
- How do you maintain a positive environment?
- Do you believe you have an environment of trust?
- Do you encourage social interaction among workers?
- How would you describe your workplace culture?
- Has your culture changed over the last five years? If so, is it better or worse?
- Do you actively work to achieve a particular type of culture or does it just happen?

### Skills Transference

- Do you encourage skills transference?
- Do you cross-pollinate within the workplace whereby employees are transferred into different departments or locations for experience and to expand their knowledge of the organization as a whole?
- Do you have a mentoring program in place?
- Do you have a coaching program in place for high-potential employees?

- Do you have a coaching program in place for employees with strong skills, but behavioral deficiencies?

## Saying Good-bye

- What procedures are in place for redundancies?
- Do you conduct exit interviews, and are they effective? Who conducts them?
- Do you outsource exit interviews to an independent party?
- Do you act on the information provided from an exit interview or ignore it?
- Do you provide departing employees with outplacement support to help them focus on tomorrow and minimize potential negative morale with remaining employees?
- Have you experienced layoffs in your organization in the past? How well did you treat people leaving, and how did the remaining employees react?
- What did you learn from the experience? Have you changed your policies as a result?
- Do you reemploy people who have been let go? If so, do other ongoing employees accept this?
- In what capacity do you reemploy them?

## Competition

- Have you researched your competition and looked at their employment policies?
- Are there any personnel from your competitors you would like to entice to join your organization?
- In which areas are your competitors better than you?
- In which areas are you better than your competitors? Can you validate this?
- What can you learn from your competitors?

---

*If we command our wealth, we shall be rich and free. If our wealth commands us, we are poor indeed.*
Edmund Burke, British Statesman & Orator

---

## The Organization

- Do you consider your organization to be an employer of choice? Can you show clear examples that support this view?
- Is there a shared vision of the employees within the organization?
- How do you maintain a positive organizational growth attitude?
- What are the areas that require further development?
- How do you monitor corporate progress?
- What can you do to be a better employer?
- Does the organization encourage an environment of constant learning? Do you consider your organization to be a "learning organization"?
- What can be done to achieve an ideal culture in the organization?

## Corporate Philosophies

- What are your workplace values?
- Are your values clearly defined and communicated to all employees?
- How do you communicate values?
- Do you embrace equal opportunity within your organization?
- Do you discriminate in any way, either overtly or covertly?
- How could you improve your organization?

### Identify Patterns and Draw Conclusions

Consider your answers to these questions carefully. What themes have emerged? Perhaps you've identified that more flexibility needs to be introduced into the workplace or that more research is required to identify who is suitable to lead your organization in the future. Do you recognize the necessary changes required to adapt successfully to your evolving workplace? What action do you need to take to prepare for the future?

There are, no doubt, some questions that stood out as being pertinent to your current situation. Also, by becoming aware of the overall status of your organization, you will have hopefully recognized the necessary actions required (which may not require much activity at all) to achieve a significant positive impact on the performance of your organization in the short-term and long-term.

Whether you are the CEO, a divisional head, a manager, or supervisor, to successfully move forward you must be prepared to make changes and evolve with those you employ. Take the time to discover what resources are available to you within the ranks of your employees and what investment is necessary to retain them and ensure that they are highly motivated. Perhaps, by addressing these questions, you will realize that the solutions to your challenges become clear.

No matter how strong you perceive your organization to be, it is always possible to continue to learn and strive to be better. Knowledge is nothing without action!

---

*Most people skate to where the puck is. I skate to where the puck is going to be.*
Wayne Gretzky, Canadian Ice Hockey Player

---

# Retain and Gain

## Winning Retention Strategies

Smart people pick organizations, not vice versa. In an economy where they are spoilt for choice, success is increasingly a question of capturing the emotions of the skilled individuals you need.

Is your company today held hostage by "core competents"— talented individuals possessing the skills that make your products and services unique? If so, you're not alone. In a study by the Corporate Leadership Council, a computer company recognized 100 core competents out of 16,000 employees; a software company had 10 out of 11,000; and a transportation group deemed 20 of its 33,000 employees truly critical to performance.

Progressively, these differences are also reflected in inequalities in compensation. Around 20 years ago, the salary difference between a typical U.S. chief executive and the average factory worker was a factor of 40:1. It now stands at more than 400:1. In 1999, Jack Welch made more money than the combined salaries of the 15,000 maquiladora workers who assembled products for GE in Mexico.

Some may say that the war for talent was a "new economy" phenomenon of the late 1990s and that today people are happy just to have a job. In the very short term, they may be right, but in the longer term there are two important counterarguments.

First, no company ever went bankrupt because it suffered from having too much talent. Recent research shows that only seven percent of all managers strongly agree with the statement "our company has enough talented managers to pursue all or most of its promising opportunities."

In addition, 75 percent of executives worldwide now rank human performance ahead of productivity and technology in terms of strategic importance. The same study also reveals that 80 percent of all executives claim that by 2010 attracting and retaining people will be the leading success factor in strategy.

Second, the pool of talent in the industrialized world will start shrinking in the years to come. Over the next decade, the number of people between 35 and 45 years old will fall by 15 percent as a proportion of the population in Europe and North America.

The high-end niche of the labor market is therefore becoming an increasingly imperfect market. Core competents will stay only as long as organizations can offer them something they desire. Bear in mind, though, that this phenomenon concerns a small group of highly skilled people. In the mainstream labor market, competition continues to rise. However, talent does not necessarily equate to an impressive title. Core competents need not be senior executives, but could just as easily be people whose intellectual property is crucial to the organization, or whose particular expertise is difficult to replicate.

"Devising Strategies to Prevent the Flight of Talent," Jonas Ridderstråle, co-author of *Funky Business* and *Karaoke Capitalism*. (Article written for *Financial Times*, London, August 27, 2002)

As available talent decreases and demand increases, more opportunities become available for individuals within the workforce which, quite simply, means employees are becoming increasingly harder to retain. Young people showing much promise may leave out of frustration, or a belief that they can progress much faster elsewhere, if they are not given the support to develop and gain valuable skills. Older people may choose to seek employment elsewhere that offers more flexibility so as to achieve their desired work/life balance.

Although it is impossible to completely control employee turnover, it is possible to be in a stronger position of successfully influencing workers to stay on by providing an attractive work environment and incentives that are aligned with each individual's desires.

Often employees are told how good they are and offered future advancement only when they submit their resignation to pursue a perceived better opportunity elsewhere. Many years back, when I was working with a major U.S. bank, I was headhunted to join a rival bank. After assessing the opportunities for the future within the new role, I decided to accept the offer. Upon presenting my resignation, the CEO and Human Resources director both advised me that another department of the organization had wanted to offer me a more senior role, but my current boss had refused to allow them to approach me. As I had already given a commitment to the new organization, I left. Perhaps if there had been an open environment to discuss my career prospects, I may not have decided to go elsewhere.

In order to retain good people, the following points should be adopted:

- Acknowledge achievements and give credit when due. Offer suitable rewards for accomplishments (people want more than just cash to stay with your company).
- Give employees honest feedback—negative and positive, to guide and assist them to better themselves.
- Give stimulating challenges whenever possible to help ensure job enjoyment and fulfillment.
- Recognize commitment and results (not just hours worked).
- Conduct a thorough skills analysis to identify training and development requirements.
- Provide continuous training/upskilling and learning.
- Encourage personal growth and creativity.
- Prepare younger workers for senior leadership roles by encouraging communication and interaction with older workers. Learn from their experience (and mistakes).
- Offer a corporate mentoring program.
- Allow flexible working styles wherever possible such as tele-conferencing, working from home, and flexible working hours.
- Share company objectives, visions, and values and be sure they are clearly understood and accepted.
- Keep employees up-to-date with company progress, performance goals, and issues.
- Promote open communication at all levels.
- Seek feedback. Ask employees to openly analyze systems and offer any suggestions for improvement. Be responsive and listen to what your workers say they want.
- Be certain that existing management are equipped for changing situations. Are they capable of positively motivating staff if conditions become difficult, for example, due to economic downturn or internal structure changes?
- Assign high-profile projects to high potentials at all levels.
- Ensure that the culture or personality of the organization fits with those you want to retain.
- Be sure the environment is friendly and welcoming.
- Encourage team interaction.
- Jointly create clear career development plans.
- Have regular honest performance appraisals.
- Assist employees to become proud of the organization they work within.

In the changing world of work, people no longer want to be told what to do, particularly tomorrow's leaders, such as Gen X and Gen Y workers. They are more likely to be motivated by having the freedom to work creatively without being micromanaged and judged by the results of their efforts.

---

*The average 34-year-old has already worked for nine different companies in his or her brief career.*
Elaine L. Chao, Secretary of Labor, U.S. Department of Labor, 2001

---

To retain productive employees, their days must be meaningful, and corporate and personal goals must be aligned in order to fit in with their desired career goals and work/life balance. An environment also needs to be created to ensure that, should they take an extended leave, they are motivated to return to the organization on an agreed-upon date in the future.

A forward-thinking lawyer friend of mine told me how an associate had taken nine months' special leave to backpack around Europe. Because the legal firm believed this young lawyer to be highly talented with much potential and promise to work his way to becoming a partner, his job had been kept open and additional incentives were provided to entice him to return. Not only did this flexible approach retain a valued, high-potential employee, it also saved the organization approximately $200,000 in lost revenue, as well as recruitment, training, and development costs if the young lawyer had to be replaced.

---

A steady and significant 80 percent of employees would prefer to advance within their current organization than change organizations to achieve the same end.

The L.E.A.D (Leadership Employment & Direction) 2003 Survey Report, Commissioned by Leadership Management Australia, conducted by Quantum Market Research

---

Flexibility must be provided wherever possible, recognizing and respecting employees' needs such as maternity leave, paternal leave, elder care leave, study time, or an extended vacation. Also, many workers may wish to undertake different roles with their employer and, at certain times, perhaps phase down their responsibilities in order to achieve their desired work/life balance.

To retain good people, to take your organization forward successfully, you must endeavor to understand their needs and desires, create a flexible work environment, and provide personal learning opportunities to enhance each individual's abilities. An employee's loyalty can no longer be taken for granted. Offering flexible employment solutions designed to suit both the organization and the individual engages people in a way that encourages them to want to come to work each day.

---

The most employable people in 2013 will be:
- Well educated. A university degree, a strong understanding of "big picture" issues that impact business. They will have the required technical skills. And they will be desirous of continuous learning.
- Soft skills will be inherent. Leadership capabilities to work in a team-based workplace culture. Effective interpersonal and communication skills. An ability to think strategically.
- A good worker who, as a self-starter, will have a desire to work hard. And who, as self-reliant, will have an ability to work smarter.
- These people, in all likelihood, will be working in Information Technology, Engineering or Sales and Marketing.

The Future of Work Survey, DBM, 2003

---

## Flexibility = Prosperity

The days of the inflexible employer are numbered. Both employers and employees must now determine a more flexible way to work and align their goals so they may prosperously work in harmony for mutual benefit. New strategies must evolve within the workplace to encompass the diverse, multigenerational workforce.

Workplace strategies, as we have known them in the past, will not be returning. We have learned over the last decade that an employer can no longer guarantee job security. (They can't even guarantee their own survival!) A "job for life" doesn't exist anymore and we are responsible for planning our own careers.

In order to retain workers, it is critical to recognize the changing needs, wants, and goals of your employees as they age. Younger employees strive to work hard (usually in a full-time capacity), build up savings, provide for their growing families, and focus on developing careers. However, some employers wrongly assume that a promise of continual promotion will guarantee maximization of retention and motivation of their younger workers, when, in fact, many prefer flexible career options.

Older employees may wish to continue up the corporate ladder, or, alternatively, work under less pressure or work fewer hours (even if it means earning less pay). Many mature workers prefer flexible working arrangements such as working part-time, job sharing, consulting, contracting, or mentoring, enabling them to achieve their desired work/life balance. Too few employers provide such flexibility.

Flexible workplace systems must be created in order to recognize the aspirations of all employees, young and experienced, to ensure greater work satisfaction, empowerment, self-fulfillment, and productivity. Necessary steps need to be taken to ensure optimum corporate profitability, performance, and responsibility.

---

*If you don't drive your business, you will be driven out of business.*
B. C. Forbes, Scottish Journalist

---

### Treating People Well

The Australian organization, Cordukes Limited (a construction and facilities management company) are currently undergoing a major transformation following a turbulent period of significant losses, where the future of the organization was seriously threatened. The recently appointed CEO, Martin Whittaker, is working hard with his team to rebuild and strengthen Cordukes and believes that building the right culture is a key competitive advantage. Although only in the early stages of recovery, Whittaker and his team are striving to become an employer of choice, an organization that people want to join and stay with.

The following report, which, I believe, encompasses valuable strategies for retaining talent and restoring confidence, was written by Whittaker and distributed and discussed with his team:

---

The organizational climate that exists in any company is best determined by asking the question "What's it like to work around here?" Do people talk positively about work? Is there a buzz or chatter of constant positive interaction, generally work related, but involving some outside work activities? Is work seen as an ongoing and integral part of employees' lives?

The way employees answer this question will be a combination of the way in which they have been treated and how they see others being treated across a range of issues. The more recent the experience, the greater will be its overall impact. Although climate is influenced by organization policies and standards, the most significant influence on climate, as perceived by an employee, is their direct supervisor.

At Cordukes Limited, we are aspiring to become an Employer of Choice. The way we treat individual employees has a significant influence on the climate created and, ultimately will determine whether we achieve our Employer of Choice aspiration.

We are a service company—we do not have tangible products. We will succeed based on the collective power of our people, the quality of the services we provide, the knowledge and skill of our people, and the way we focus those capabilities in the marketplace.

Skillfully harnessing our people can be our greatest competitive advantage. In the market place, competitors can copy prices almost immediately. They can replicate a new product or process within a year. However, environments or climates take years to build up and, without the right leaders in place, they will be impossible to copy.

The right climate is one that attracts people, allows them to flourish, and makes them want to stay.

As a guide to the way in which we want our people to be treated, the core values of the company represent an appropriate starting place. We spent some time defining these values and they are very important:

**People**—We will develop and maintain successful relationships with our team. We will look after their safety.
**Learning**—We learn by asking people what they think and by explaining decisions.
**Integrity**—We do what we say and are always honest and fair.
**Fulfillment**—We fulfill our team's needs through listening, understanding, problem solving, and meeting needs/expectations.
**Stewardship**—We accept ownership, responsibility, and accountability for the actions we take and encourage the same of others.

If we can foster this kind of climate and ultimately achieve it—and it does take a long time—then I have a deep conviction that our organization will be successful no matter what it does.

Martin Whittaker, CEO, Cordukes Limited, Australia, September 2003

## Move Forward and Conquer

---

*There is no security in this life. There is only opportunity.*
General Douglas MacArthur

---

As we realize the future of work is going to continuously evolve, we need to plan now to ensure our corporate preservation and prosperity. This is a world that is changing fast, and inefficient companies applying outdated concepts will be gobbled up or will perish. Where does your organization aspire to go, and what talent and skills are required to achieve your desired results?

As mature workers and baby boomers approach retirement, we must not only adapt our work environment to entice younger workers to join and remain with our organizations, but identify the experienced workers who can make healthy contributions and encourage them to stay on flexible terms and dissuade them from departing for early retirement.

Many organizations have failed because they have overlooked long-term planning. Particularly over the last decade, pressure from investors, funds managers, the media, and bankers has been on optimizing short-term performance. The net result is that many organizations have not fulfilled their potential, as long-term strategies have been abandoned or modified. In order to be sure that short-term goals are achieved (and therefore guarantee the CEO's survival), shareholders have ultimately been penalized through substandard short-term strategies. Those who have endured the tough times, successfully address both short-term and long-term performance to ensure ongoing survival.

---

Today's competitive advantage can evaporate tomorrow—because the world is full of competitors trying to market newer, better products and services to replace yours. People who continuously learn and build new skills are the source of sustainable competitive advantage. They meet challenges with continuous improvement and invent whole new approaches and processes. The most successful organizations cultivate many people who can continually learn and improve. Organizations with only a few who can do this can't keep up with competitive challenges. Their survival is at risk.

That makes managers with the skills to inspire continuous learning in their people the most critical strategic asset of any organization that operates in a tough, competitive marketplace. To sustain its edge, an